Disaster in the Air :
The Crash of the Kashmir Princess 1955

Disaster in the Air :
The Crash of the Kashmir Princess 1955

Colonel A.K. Mitra

RELIANCE PUBLISHING HOUSE
NEW DELHI (INDIA)

All rights reserved. No part of this publication may be reproduced, stored, in a retrieval system, or transmitted in any from or by any means, electronic, mechanical, photocopying, recording, or otherwise, without the prior permission of Reliance Publishing House.

First Published 2017

ISBN : 81-7510-123-7

Price: Rs. 350

Published by :
Reliance Publishing House
3026/7H, Ranjit Nagar,
New Delhi-110008.
Ph. : 5737377/5722605
Fax: 5744673/5772748

Composed by :
Geeta Graphics
J 436, Baljeet Nagar,
New Delhi-110008.
Ph. 5715330

Printed by :
S.S.S.Printers
New Delhi.

DEDICATION

To my beloved grandson

DEBARYA (JOY) DUTTA - 1974-2000

"Do not be dismayed at a parting,
for a farewell is necessary
before we can meet again ...."

From the moment he came into this world, until a cruel twist of fate made him bid farewell, (the crash of Alliance Air Boeing 737 at Patna, Bihar, India at 0730 hrs, 17th July, 2000) Debarya brought immense happiness to all whose lives he touched. For this, and more, he was aptly called...

"JOY"

He will, forever, live on in our hearts.
This book is dedicated to his memory.

A.K. Mitra

FOREWORD

by

Major General D. K. Palit, VrC, F.R.G.S.

It is not often that one comes across an international mystery thriller at the highest level of world leaders, a sort of super-who-dunnit in this case featuring President Soekarno of Indonesia and Prime Ministers Nehru and Chou-en Lai of India and Communist China in a dastardly act of mass murder. The incident I refer to is the act of sabotage that caused the crash of the chartered Air-India International Super-Constellation, The *Kashmir Princess,* carrying a party of Communist Chinese journalists to the first Non-aligned Summit Conference at Bandung, Indonesia, in April 1955.

The case was solved because of the meticulous investigation carried out by an Inquiry Commission appointed by the Government of Indonesia, and the co-operation freely offered by Air India officials, British officials in Hong Kong and by ships of the Royal Navy and the Navy of Indonesia.

The occasion for the publication of this book, so many years after the event, is that my old and valued Regimental friend, Colonel A. K. Mitra (late of Ninth Gorkha Rifles) and at that time serving as the Military, Naval and Air Attache in the Indian Embassy in Djakarta, was the Indian member of the Inquiry Commission. Having met him in Delhi after some years, I was able to persuade him to dig into his old papers (and into the recesses of his memory) to write an account of that incident.

In 1955, both India and Indonesia were newcomers to the international comity of free nation states — some-what green around the edges and not yet inured to the polity of international skullduggery. This "new Asia" was still innocent of the ruthlessness of the "dirty tricks" departments of the C.I.A. (or M.I.6 and other western Intelligence agencies); and the realisation that an unarmed, civilian air liner carrying non-belligerents could be deliberately destroyed in mid-flight in order to prevent Communist China's participation in a non-aligned conference, caused a sense of revulsion and horror among Asian peoples.

"A.K." has given us a very interesting account, combining accurate reportage of an official investigation with his personal knowledge of the men and events concerned — all served up with a fluent style. A good read.

(D. K. Palit)
Major General

PREFACE

Any person who has led an active life, either in civilian government service or in the defence services or in a company or running his own business or as an independent professional, will find it very difficult to keep himself occupied after his retirement. He suddenly finds time hanging heavily upon him. To escape the boredom of retired life, many people take up some hobby (even during their active service career) such as collecting stamps or coins or gardening or writing poetry or doing some social service. With every passing year the retired man suffers from greater infirmities, frailties and the pains of old age but even then he feels a compelling urge to do something useful.

I am now in my eighties; and I also felt a compelling urge to do something useful. As I was pondering what I should do, it suddenly struck me — why not write about some interesting events, incidents, anecdotes and experiences of my career in the army and later in the diplomatic service ! During my active service career, I had developed the habit of maintaining a diary making brief notes of day to day events, regardless of whether they were trivial or important, preserving newspaper cuttings and photographs of important events and personalities. Also, I am fortunate to be endowed with a good memory. I thus had the basic material to draw upon. As I was mulling over what I should write about, it suddenly occurred to me — why not write about the crash of the ill-fated *Kashmir Princess,* Air-India's Super Constellation airliner which had been chartered by the Government of the People's Republic of China to send the advance party of their delegation from Hong Kong to Djakarta to attend the first Afro-Asian conference which was held in Bandung, Indonesia in April 1955. As the Military, Naval and Air Attache in the Indian Embassy in Djakarta, during the period 1953-1956, I had been nominated as the accredited representative of the Government of India to the Inquiry Commission set up by the Government of Indonesia to investigate into the causes of the crash of the ill-fated aircraft in

Indonesian waters on April 11, 1955. Having made up my mind that I would write about the crash, I began a frantic search to locate my old memorabilia. This led to the discovery of an old steel trunk dumped in the loft in my garage. I had a hunch that this old trunk might contain my old collection. On opening the trunk, I found an old tattered cardboard box inside which, I found, to my delight and relief, my old diaries, notes, newspaper cuttings and photographs. I found these old records to be moth-eaten and almost crumbling. With great care, I emptied out the contents of the box and started working on them to prevent further damage, I then set about writing about that period of my service career, that is 1954-1956, and this book is the outcome.

Even though I had had an urge to do something useful, but for the constant encouragement of my good friend and colleague in the regiment of 9 Gorkha Rifles Major General D.K. Palit, VrC, affectionately called "Monty", this story might not have seen the light of day. Apart from encouraging me to take up the project of writing this story, Monty made it worth my while to undertake this project by making a generous monetary grant for the project work from the General Palit Military Studies Trust, monitored by the Institute of Defence Studies and Analysis, New Delhi. I would like to express my grateful thanks to Monty for his encouragement, magnanimity and generosity.

I knew that the manuscript of this story, running into about 150 pages, needed a second look in order to make the narrative interesting and readable, The editing of the manuscript was ably handled by M.Gopal Rao (Gopi to all of us), a very dear family friend. I would like to thank him for his valuable assistance.

The oil painting on the cover page of this book is a beautiful piece of work by my very dear friend Colonel Jitendra Hazarika, late of Army Engineers. I would like to express my profound thanks to my dear friend for an excellent pictorial representation of a plane crash.

Last but not the least, my wife Neela, who was very closely associated with the first family of Indonesia (Dr. Soekarno and his family) during that period (1954-1956) has contributed her patience and encouragement. This book, as also several other things which make for domestic bliss, would otherwise not have been possible.

Before I close, would tike to express my thanks to Naveen Rampal, student of Indusrtial Designing - IIT Delhi, for his help for organizing typing of the entire manuscript on the computer and putting them together in proper shape.

NOIDA
September, 2000 **A. K. MITRA**

CONTENTS

		Page No.
	Foreword by *Major General D.K.Palit Vrc. F.R.G.S.*	vii-viii
	Preface by *Colonel A.K. Mitra*	ix-xi

Chapters

1.	Indonesia in the Fifties	1-4
2.	Glimpses of Djakarta, Bogor and Bandung	5-9
3.	The historic Bogor and Bandung Conferences	11-13
4.	Disaster in the air - The Crash of the Kashmir Princess	21-27
5.	Inquiry Commission Interviews eyewitnesses	31-35
6.	What the Survivors had to say	37-60
7.	Fact-finding in Singapore and Djakarta	63-84
8.	The Salvage of the Wreckage	87-92
9.	The Mystery of the Crash Unravelled at Hong Kong	101-108
10.	The Commission's Findings	109-114
11.	Tributes to the Victims, the Survivors and the Rescuers	117-118

LIST OF ANNEXURES

Annexure No.			Page No.
1.		Map : Republic of Indonesia	4
2.		Map : Bogor Conference - December 1954	14
3.		Photograph : The Bogor Palace	15
4.	A	Photograph : Prime Ministers of India and Burma arrive in Djakarta (Dec 27, 1954) to attend the Bogor Conference.	16
	B	Photograph : Prime Minister Nehru being received by Mr. Tyabji, Indian Ambassador at Djakarta and welcomed by the family members and children of the staff of the Indian Embassy, Djakarta (Dec 27, 1954)	17
5.	A	Photograph : Mass meeting (Dec 30. 1954) at Ikada Stadium, Djakarta in honour of the five visiting Prime Ministers.	18
	B	Photograph : lunch hosted by Mr. Tyabji, Indian Ambassador at Djakarta, at his residence (Dec 30, 1954) in honour of Prime Minister Nehru.	19
6.		Photograph : Lockheed Super Constellation aircraft-VT-DEP-*The Kashmir Princess* of Air India International in flight.	28
7.		Map : Planned flight route of Flight No. 301/29, VT-DEP (The Kashmir Princess) April 11, 1955	29
8.		Map : Area of Search to locate the wreckage of The Kashmir Princess	30

9.	Photograph : Description of various parts of the Aircraft	61
10.	Newspaper cutting : Examination of Mr. J.C.Pathak, Flight Navigator of the Kashmir Princess at Dum Dum Airport, Calcutta (April 20, 1955)	62
11.	Photocopy of Note dated April 18, 1955 (Camp : Bandung) sent by Prime Minister Nehru to Mr. Tyabji	85
12.	Newspaper cutting : Arrival of the Members of the Inquiry Commision at Singapore.	86
13.	Newspaper cutting : Body of Captain Jatar being brought to Singapore.	93
14. A	Photograph : Wreckage of The Kashmir Princess - Front and Port side - Cockpit section	94
B	Photograph : Top & Starboard Side	95
15. A	Photograph : Starboard Wing	96
B	Photograph : Outer Wing Bottom Side Starboard Wing	97
16. A	Photograph : The twisted, burnt and corroded parts of the clockwork Timed infernal Machine	98
B	Photograph : The Clockwork Mechanism	99
17.	Newspaper cutting : Regarding the communique of the Ministry of Communications, Govt. of Indonesia and the Findings of the Inquiry Commission.	115
18.	Photocopy : Text of address delivered by Mr. Tyabji at Negara Palace, Djakarta on February 22, 1956 (3 pages)	119
19.	Newspaper cutting : Regarding the ceremony at the President's Palace in Djakarta on February 22, 1956, with an Illustration of both sides of the Medallion	122

20.	A	Photograph : The five Indonesian Islanders who rescued the three survivors of the crash of The Kashmir Princess.	123
	B	Photograph : Mr. Tyabji presenting specially-struck medallions and cash awards to the Indonesian Islanders from Natuna Islands at the President's Palace, Djakarta.	124
21.		Photograph : Col. A.K.Mitra and Mrs. Neela Mitra with Dr. Soekarno at the Palace	125

Chapter 1

INDONESIA IN THE FIFTIES

Indonesia is the largest archipelago in the world. comprising five main islands viz- Java, Sumatra, Borneo (Kalimantan), Celebes and Western New Guinea; 15 medium sized islands, 3000 small islands which are inhabited and many hundreds of tiny islands which are not inhabited. If one were to look at Indonesia from a spaceship it might perhaps give the impression of a large land mass having been blown to pieces and scattered over a wide area by the detonation of an atom bomb!

Essentially Indonesia is a long string of volcanoes interspersed by fertile plains. While the principal occupation in the island of Java is agriculture, equatorial rain forests cover most of the islands of Sumatra, Borneo, Celebes and Western New Guinea, making communications difficult. With its vast unexploited reserves of oil and minerals, the island of Sumatra offers the maximum scope for development and is regarded as the future hope of Indonesia. The archipelago has rainfall for almost seven months in a year, with an annual average of 80 ". The climate, in general, being hot and humid, is enervating and not conducive to sustained hard work

The estimated population of Indonesia in the 1950s was about 78 million, with the highest density on the island of Java (about 50 million). Though larger in size, Sumatra had a population of about 10 million. The other islands including the large islands ot Borneo, Celebes and Western New Guinea, were thinly populated.

The Chinese population, 2.5 million at that time, constituted the largest foreign ethnic group in Indonesia. As the main middle class group of traders and small businessman, it was the backbone of the economy. However, politically-conscious Indonesians, who were aware of the emergence of communist China as a powerful Communist State, viewed with suspicion the loyalty of the local Chinese and considered them a menace to the security of the country. The section of the local Chinese who were supposed to be the agents of Nationalist China (Formosa), were viewed with even greater suspicion and resentment. There was a growing feeling, even amongst ordinary villagers, that the Chinese, an unassimilated ethnic group, were preying on the local economy.

Besides the Chinese, there were a few thousand other Asians predominantly well-to-do Sindhis and South Indian Muslims engaged in small businesses and a few thousand Europeans and Eurasians who were regarded with distrust and dislike. At that time, over 90% of the population of Indonesia was Muslim. Indonesia is the largest Islamic nation in the world, but without the fundamentalist fanaticism found in most other Islamic states. On the contrary, it is a true synthesis of ancient religions and cultures - mostly Hindu, Buddhist and Islam. The Indonesian Muslims were, on the whole, tolerant and genuinely desirous of evolving as a secular state like India. Nationalism, secularism and economic liberalism were the key notes of the Nationalist Party (PNI) founded by President Soekarno, of which Dr. Ali Sastraamidjojo was also one of the original leaders.

Under the leadership of Soekarno. the Indonesians fought bloody guerila wars against the Dutch and eventually gained their independence in August 1945. However, unlike the British rulers of India, the Dutch rulers of Indonesia had not created adequate facilities for education nor had they provided opportunities to the Indonesian people to participate in the civil administration of the country. As a result, when the Indonesians took charge of their country in August 1945, they lacked the administrative skills required to govern and administer a country. The Indonesian economy deteriorated gradually and by 1950, the country was facing a severe economic crisis and the threat of a military coup.

In the early 1950's, the economic ills of the country, a weak and inefficient administration. squabbles among the political parties, inefficiency and the lack of discipline in the armed forces which tended to meddle in politics, the presence of a large Chinese population whose loyalty to the country was suspect - all these factors appeared to motivate the Communist party in its bid to capture political power in the country.

As the first President of Indonesia, Soekarno was fully aware of the dangers looming on the horizon. He possessed the invaluable gift of oratory ; the sheer power of his words was enough to mesmerise the masses, inspire them and to arouse their nationalist fervour. President Soekarno was the author of the concept of " Guided Democracy " as practiced in Indonesia during his presidentship. This helped him retain his influence and control over the political fortunes of the country and over the army. However, all his etlorts to bring down the inflation rate and to revive the economy appeared to be of no avail.

Soekarno was anxious to secure the support and, possibly, economic aid from friendly neighboring countries in order to bail out the Indonesian economy. He was able to persuade the Prime Ministers of

Indonesia in the Fifties

Burma, Ceylon, India and Pakistan (the so-called Colombo Powers) to agree to hold the first conference of the Colombo Plan countries at Bogor (Indonesia) in December 1954. At this conference, the Prime Ministers discussed the agenda for the proposed (first).Afro-Asian Conference which was to be held in April 1955 at Bandung as well as to decide on the countries to be invited. The main item on the agenda was the promotion of economic co-operation, trade, education and cultural exchanges among the participating Afro-Asian countries. One of the historic decisions taken at the Bogor Conference was to invite Communist China to the Afro-Asian Conference. Most of the Afro-Asian countries had democratic governments and therefore this decision was greatly resented by the western countries, in particular U.S.A.

The Bogor and Bandung Conferences helped to improve the image and increase the prestige of Indonesia and to boost the morale of the Indonesian people. Soekarno temporarily regained his popularity and thereby achieved his aim.

Politics in Indonesia at that time appeared to be in the melting pot; it seemed that personalities counted for more than principles. There were then four outstanding personalities in Indonesian politics viz. President Dr. Soekarno, Vice President Dr. Mohmed Hatta, the socialist leader Sultan Sjarir and the Sultan of Jogjakarta. They appeared to be pulling in different directions because of personal squabbles. even though there seemed to be a broad similarity in their political ideas.

As Supreme Commander of the armed forces and with his charismatic personality and great power of his oratory, Soekarno was able to avert any major political crisis in the country. He was one of the renowned scholars of his time and, among other things, possessed a profound knowledge of Indian history, culture, literature and the story of India's freedom struggle.

At that time, the armed forces in Indonesia lacked tradition, discipline and central control and guidance. They were disorganized, ill-equipped and ill-paid; and they were actively participating in the political life of the country. Indonesia occupied (and continues to occupy) a strategic position in South-East Asia and it was therefore desirable that the country be politically stable and militarily strong in order to maintain internal law and order and to prevent foreign infiltration. It was also desirable that the armed forces remain above party politics in the interests of a stable democratic government. The Indonesian people had intense national pride and were extremely sensitive to any patronizing by other nations. Unfortunately, the economic policies pursued by President Soekarno inexorably plunged the nation into a severe economic crisis and rampant

4   *Disaster in the Air : The Crash of the Kashmir Princess 1955*

inflation; and his policy of promoting friendly relationships with China led to a decline in his popularity in later years. In 1967, General Suharto ousted Soekarno as President and established a new order. He succeeded in restoring economic stability in the country.

Dr. Achmad Soekarno, the first President of the Republic of Indonesia, who suffered and fought for his country and eventually gained freedom from Dutch rule in August 1945, died in 1970. It was a great pity that at the time of his death he was denied a funeral befitting his role as the architect of Indonesia's freedom and as the builder of a secular democracy in Indonesia.

ANNEXURE - 1

Republic of Indonesia

Chapter 2

GLIMPSES OF DJAKARTA, BOGOR AND BANDUNG

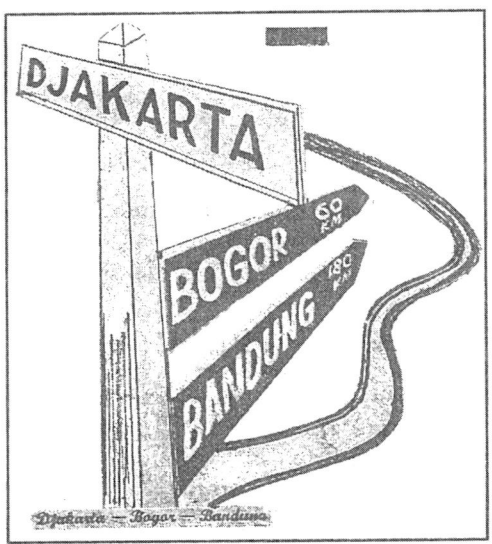

Djakarta

Djakarta is the capital of the republic of Indonesia. In the l6th century, before the Dutch came to Indonesia, on the site of the present Djakarta stood the harbour town of Sunda Kelepa, the chief port for the Sundanese Kingdom of Padjadjaran. Trading used to be carried out from this port initially with the Portuguese and later with the Dutch merchants. At that time, Sunda Kelepa was ruled by the Sultan of Bautam who allowed the Dutch to land in his territory at the end of the 16th century. It was the Sultan of Bautam who changed the name of Sunda Kelepa to "DJAKARTA" which meant "GLORIOUS FORTRESS". He also allowed the Dutch to establish their trading centre at Djakarta.

The Sultan called for help from the British when he found that the Dutch had converted their trading centre into a fortress but betore the British could render any assistance, the Dutch, with their superior force, first burnt down the British trading post and then razed Djakarta to the ground, renaming the place as Batavia. Eventually, the Dutch East India Company took over the administration and gradually built a new township, protected by a surrounding wall and a fortress on the shore.

The Chinese, numbering about 1000 at that time, were allowed by the Dutch to live within the walled city since they were the tradesmen, tailors, carpenters and others performing various utility services. They were classed as a separate section of the population. The native indonesians were made to live outside the walled city, in the countryside covered with tropical rainforest. (The Indonesians comprised people from different parts of the Archipelago except the Javanese). They were not allowed to settle down near the walled city for the Dutch feared attacks by them. During the 17th century, Batavia became the trading centre of the region. Goods were imported from Persia, India and Japan and the rest of Indonesia into their warehouses for trading abroad.

In 1732, a severe malarial epidemic took a heavy toll of life, making Batavia an extremely unhealthy place to live in. As a result, the Governor General of the Dutch East India Company decided to move his residence to Bogor. In the subsequent period, Batavia underwent many changes, The population increased and became more heterogeneous with the influx of people from the unsettled Sultanates, from nearby Malaya and with the assimilation of some British and Portuguese merchants. Some relics of the past can still be found, such as the remains of a Church built around 1695 and an old town hall dating back to 1710. In the thickly populated Glodok area, the Chinese lived in unhygienic conditions with their dwellings crowded together on the banks of old canals.

Djakarta has played an important part in the history of Indonesia's struggle for independence. Before the Second World War, most of the organisations of the independence movement had their headquarters in Djakarta. The Dutch rulers took harsh measures to suppress and to break up the growing menace of the independence movement. Djakarta had also been the centre of the Indonesian independence movement against the Japanese regime. It was in Djakarta, during the Japanese occupation, that Dr. Soekarno enunciated "PANTJASILA", the five democratic principle upon which the Indonesian State was to be based. Soon after the Japanese surrender, Indonesia was proclaimed independent - on August 17, 1945.

Bogor

Bogor is situated directly south of Djakarta, lying at the foot of the mountains. In 1745, this ancient city was renamed "BULTENZORG" by the Dutch though the people of Indonesia always refer it by its original name. It lies on a plateau about 870 feet above sea level and has a cool climate, the average mean temperature being about 25°C (about 78° F). The average annual rainfall is very high — it rains almost every day. Above the city, to the south, rises the volcanic peaks of Mount Salak and to the south-east are the twin peaks of Pangrango and Geden- more than 10,000 feet above sea level. While the twin peaks are still active, the Salak is an extinct volcano. On the plains to the north of Bogor, there are rubber and tea plantations and rice is cultivated in the neighbouring areas. In 1950, the common population of the city was about 112,600. Bogor is connected to Djakarta (a distance of 35 miles) both by good motorable roads and by an electric railway.

During the Dutch regime, the Dutch built fine palaces in Bogor but they were destroyed by severe earthquakes in 1882. The palace, now commonly known as "Bogor Residence' was built during 1856. It was at the Bogor Residence that the first conference of the Prime Ministers of the Colombo Plan countries (i.e. Ceylon, Burma, India and Pakistan and Indonesia) was held in December 1954.

Bandung

Bandung is the common name for a regency, a district and a city. The regency of Bandung covers an area of about 1,175 square miles and is a plateau with an average height of well over 2,000 feet above sea level. Geologically, it was the bed of a great lake surrounded by mountain ranges. To the south, the volcanic peaks of the South Preanger Highlands rise to heights of about 8,500 feet. The regency of Bandung is sub-divided into ten districts. The population of the whole region has registered a steep increase during the last twenty years. As per the census of October 1952, the population was then about 684,600. By the end of October 1954, the population had increased by almost seven times that figure.

Bandung city is the capital of the Province of West Java, lying on the Djakarta-Tjilatjap Railway line. It is a clean city with tree-lined avenues and streets, parks and gardens and has a cool climate. It is recognised as a holiday and tourist resort. With its scenic beauty and cool climate and well-developed transport and communication facilities, Bandung was the obvious choice of the Indonesian Government as the venue for the first Afro-Asian Conference which was to be held in April 1955.

The most frequent references in this story will be to the districts of Djakarta, Bogor and Bandung. Djakarta is the capital of Indonesia; Bogor is the scientific centre some 60 km from Djakarta; Bandung was the location of international conferences held earlier; and now the First Afro-Asian Conference was scheduled to be held in April 1955.

The Episode at Hotel D'zan, Djakarta

It is not unusual for any person arriving in a foreign country for the first time, to feel lost. Everything seems so strange and different - the language, the way of life, the currency. It takes time to get used to one's new surroundings and to settle down to a new routine. This was how I felt when I first landed in Djakarta in July 1953.

The first conference of the Prime Ministers of the Colombo Plan countries was held in Bogor at the end of December 1954, Mr. Krishna Menon attended as Adviser to the Ministry of External Affairs, Govt. of India. His accommodation had been arranged in Hotel D'zan, the only five star hotel in Djakarta at that time. In those days, the hotel staff and the bearers and attendants in the hotel spoke Dutch or Bhasha Indonesia and could hardly speak or understand any other language.

Mr. Krishna Menon, as most people know, was addicted to tea and consumed several cups a day. Soon after settling down in the hotel, Mr. Krishna Menon rang the bell and ordered tea. In a short while, a hotel bearer brought in a tray containing a teapot and a tea cup. Mr Menon looked at the tray and enquired in English as to why there was no milk or sugar. The bearer, who spoke and understood Bhasha Indonesia only, replied in his language, saying "Susu, Tuan". Mr. Menon retorted " What the bloody hell are you saying ?" To this, the bearer replied in his language, saying "Gula". Mr. Menon lost his temper and called the manager. Meanwhile, the bearer added to Menon's vocabulary a new word - "Salah" - and ran away in fear. Mr. Menon was quite put out when the manager, a Dutch, came in. Mr. Menon complained to the manager that the bearer had used foul words such as "Susu", "Gula" and "Salah" and demanded to know if that was the way a guest was treated in that hotel.

The embarrassed manager profusely apologised to Mr Menon for the inconvenience caused to him and politely explained to him that in Indonesia, the people did not take tea with milk or sugar, as was the practice in Britain or other Commonwealth countries. The manager added: "Sir, pardon me, in Indonesian language, "Susu" means 'Milk' and "Gula" means "Sugar" and the word "Salah" was not an offensive word but meant "Sorry, I have made a mistake".

Thereafter, the Indian Embassy in Djakarta, where I had been posted as the Military, Naval and Air Attache. made me responsible for looking after the Indian guests staying at that hotel. I went to Mr. Krishna Menon's room to make a courtesy call, when he opened the door and said : " Oh ! General, you have come" I said : "Sorry, Sir, I am only a Colonel ". To this, Mr. Menon said in a jovial manner : " Oh! No, for me, you are a General". I said : "Thank you Sir". He then narrated the entire incident and asked "What sort of language is this Bhasha Indonesia" ? Thereafter, as long as he was in Djakarta, I made arrangements to send him a big flask with tea from my house, which pleased him immensely.

Chapter 3

THE HISTORIC BOGOR AND BANDUNG CONFERENCES

An Indian Air Force Dakota brought the Indian delegation led by Prime Minister Nehru, accompanied by Dr. Mahmud, Mr. V. K. Krishna Menon and senior Indian officials, along with Prime Minister U Nu of Burma, to Kemajoran Airport in Djakarta on Monday December 27. On arrival at Djakarta, the Indian Delegation was received at the airport by Indonesian protocol officials, officials of the Indonesian Ministiy of External Affairs and members of the Indian Embassy, accompanied by their families.

Prime Ministers Nehru of India, Mohammed Ali of Pakistan, Sir John Kotlewala of Ceylon, U Nu of Burma and Prime Minister Dr. Ali Sastroamidjojo of Indonesia met at the Governor's Residence at Bogor (popularly known as "Bogor Residence") from 28th to 30th December 1954, under the chairmanship of President Soekarno. Among other matters, the Conference deliberated upon basic issues such as the venue and date for the proposed first Afro-Asian Conference and the countries to be invited. It was decided that the first Afro-Asian Conference would be held on Monday April 18, 1955 at the Governor's Palace in Bandung. The Bogor Conference further decided that the People's Republic of China should be invited to participate in the first AfroAsian Conference. It was agreed to set up a Joint Secretariat at Bandung at the earliest, consisting of experts from the sponsoring countries to work out the details of the organisation, to conduct the proposed Conference, to constitute committees for various purposes and the modalities of the conference; as well as to monitor the progress and to keep the Prime Ministers of the sponsoring countries informed of the progress. The Joint Secretariat was established at Bandung itself and started functioning from early 1955.

The people of Indonesia were filled with a sense of national pride on learning that the historic First Afro-Asian Conference would be held in their country. They were eagerly looking forward to see the leaders of the Afro-Asian countries accompanied by their delegations and to welcome them on their arrival in Indonesia. They started making preparations in right earnest to extend their warm hospitality to every single visitor from the Afro-Asian countries. The various ministries of the Government of

Indonesia such as External Affairs, Home. Civil Aviation. Press and Publicity, Culture and other Departments were busy in their respective fields to make the first Afro-Asian Confereuce a grand success and to ensure that every single visitor had a comfortable, pleasant and a memorable stay in Indonesia. The Tourism Department of the Government of Indonesia made arrangements for the leaders and members of the official delegations to visit various places of interest such as Bali Islands, Sumatra, Borneo and historical sites such as Borobadur.

In Djakarta, the people in general were eagerly looking forward to see Mr Chou en-Lai, the Prime Minister of the People's Republic of China, who was to start from Peking in a chartered Air India plane and arrive at Djakarta ahead of Mr. Nehru, the Indian Prime Minister. Initially, this plane was scheduled to go back to Rangoon (Burma) to pick up Mr. Nehru, Mr. Gamal Abdel Nasser President of Egypt, Burmese Prime Minister U Nu and the Deputy Prime Minister of Afghanistan, along with other Ministers and officials and arrive at Djakarta on April 16. Prime Minister Nehru along with the Indian Delegation was to start from New Delhi in an IAF Dakota and reach Rangoon on April 16.

The Air India plane chartered by the Chinese Government was a Lockheed Constellation Aircraft named Kashmir Princess. According to the original plan, this aircraft was to carry the advance party of the Chinese delegation for the Afro-Asian conference from Hong Kong, starting on the morning on April 11 and was to land in Djakarta the same evening. The advance party consisted of eight officials of the Government of the People's Republic of China, two Polish Journalists and one North Vietnamese official. Unfortunately, this plane crashed into the South China Sea off the Great Natuna Islands of Indonesia at about 1755 hours on Monday April 1 1, 1955, as a result of an act of sabotage perpetrated at Hong Kong Airport prior to the plane's departure. (That the plane crash was due to an act of sabotage at Hong Kong Airport was established by subsequent investigation).

The news of the plane crash in the territorial waters of Indonesia came as a rude shock to the people of Indonesia who were eagerly looking forward to the historic event, the first Afro-Asian Conference, taking place in their country. There was great gloom throughout the country.

The Government of the People's Republic of China chartered another Air India plane, this time a Skymaster, which landed at Peking on April 12. The plane took off from Peking on Wednesday April 13, carrying Mr. Chou en-Lai, the Chinese Prime Minister and other members of the Chinese Delegation and landed, if memory serves, at the Burmese border town of Muse. The Delegation consisted of ten senior members and also Shaikh Nur Mohammed, Adviser and Wang Cho Jin, Secretary General . From Burma, the Chinese Delegation was accompanied by the Burmese Ambassador to China, Mr. U Hla Maung, and the Indonesian Ambassador to China Mr. A. Mononutu. Mr. Chou en-Lai, who joined the party at Burma, arrived at Djakarta in the evening on April 13 (without any prior announcement or reception ceremony at the air port !)

The Indian Prime Minister Mr. Jawahar Lal Nehru, accompanied by Mr Gamal Abdel Nasser, President of the Republic of Egypt, U Nu, Prime Minister of Burma, Mr. Krishna Menon , Foreign Minister of India and several senior officials and members of the respective countries, arrived by another Air India Constellation on Saturday April 16, at the Kemajoran Airport, Djakarta.

ANNEXURE-2

The Historic Bogor and Bandung Conferences

ANNEXURE - 3

ANNEXURE - 4(A)

FOR BOGOR CONFERENCE

Monday 27th December, 1954 : The Prime Minister of India Pt. Jawaharlal Nehru with the Prime Minister of Burma U. Nu and staff from both countries arrived by Indian Airforce Dakota Aircraft at Kamajoran Airport Djakarta. Received by Prime Minister of Indonesia Dr. Ali Sastroamidjojo and members of Indian Embassy.

ANNEXURE - 4 (B)

Members of Indian Embassy, consisting of the Indian Ambassador Mr. Tyabji, standing just behind Mrs. Mitra, her daughter Aesha; Adil and Laila, son and daughter of Mr. Tyabji and other members of Indian Embassy, received the Prime Minister at the airport.

ANNEXURE-5(A)

Mass Meeting at Ikada Stadium, Djakarta on Thursday, 30 December 1954 at 9 a.m. in honour of five visiting Prime Ministers, President Soekarno Presided

From Left : Pakistan Prime Minister & Mrs. Mohammed Ali, Prime Minister of Burma & Mrs. U.Nu, President & Madame Soekarno, Dr. Hatta, Vice President, Mr. Nehru Prime Minister of India and Sir John Kotlewala, Prime Minister of Ceylone and other invited guests.

ANNEXURE - 5 (B)

Lunch at Mr. & Mrs. Tyabji's residence on 30 December at 12.30 A.M. in honour of Pt. Nehru.
Standing: Prime Minister's Secretary, Mrs. Sudarsono, Mrs. Tyabji, Mr. Tyabji, Mr. S. Dutt, Secretary General Ministry of External Affairs New Delhi, Colonel Mitra.
Sitting: Mr. Krishna Menon, Sutan Sjahrir - Ex-Prime Minister of Indonesia, Mr. Nehru, Mrs. Sjahrir, Dr. Mohamud of India **On Ground**: Mr. Vaidyanath, Mrs. Narendra Nath, Mrs. Mitra, Mrs. Vaidyanath and Mr. Narendra Nath.

Chapter 4

DISASTER IN THE AIR : THE CRASH OF THE *KASHMIR PRINCESS*

The Government of the Peoples' Republic of China had decided to charter an Air India plane to take the Chinese Premier Mr. Chou en-Lai and other members of the Chinese Delegation to the first Afro-Asian Conference, from Peking to Djakarta. The Chinese Premier was scheduled to arrive at Djakaita earlier than the Indian Premier Mr Nehru. According to the original schedule, this plane was to go from Djakarta to Rangoon to pick up the Indian Premier Mr. Nehru along with the members of the Indian delegation (who were scheduled to fly on April 16, 1955 from New Delhi to Rangoon by an IAF Dakota), the Egyptian President Mr. Gamal Abdel Nasser, the Burmese Premier U Nu, the Deputy Prime Minister of Afghanistan and other ministers and officials, and proceed from Rangoon to Djakarta on April 16.

The Chinese Govemment changed its plan at the last moment having got information that there was a plot to harass the members of their Delegation either on the way to the Hong Kong airport or at the airport itself. They decided to send an advance party of the Chinese delegation consisting of eight officials of the Chinese Government, two journalists from Poland and one North Vietnamese official in the chartered Air India plane which was scheduled to land at Hong Kong airport on the morning on April 11 and take off from there after about an hour, reaching Djakarta the same evening at about 1800 hours.

The Air India plane (Lockheed Constellation) chartered by the Chinese Government and used by it to send the advance party of their delegation to Djakarta was The *Kashmir Princess.*

The *Kashmir Princess* took off from the Santa Cruz Air Port, Bombay, on the aftemoon of Sunday April 10 for Hong Kong, via Calcutta and Bangkok. There was a change of crew at Bangkok airport. The names of the members of the new crew were as follows :

1. Mr. Damodar Kashinath Jatar - Captain.
2. Mr. Mahesh Chandra Dikshit - Co-Pilot
3. Mr. J.C. Pathak - Flight Navigator.

4. Mr. K.F.D' Cunha - Flight Engineer.
5. Mr. C. D'Souza - Flight Purser.
6. Mr. J. J. Primento - Flight Purser.
7. Miss Gloria Berry - Air Hostess.
8. Mr. Anant Shridar Karnik - Aircraft Maintenance Engineer.

All the members of the crew possessed adequate experience and the relevant licenses, for performing the duties assigned to them. Captain Jatar was one of the most senior pilots of Air India International Corporation and had to his credit over 12,300 hours of flying time, including 4,900 hours as commander of the Constellation type of aircraft.

The *Kashmir Princess* was fully air-worthy and properly certified. The flight from Bombay to Bangkok was smooth and without incidents. She took off from Bangkok airport after midnight of April 10 and landed at Hong Kong airport at about 1100 hours on April 11. Captain Jatar was anxious to take off from Hong Kong Airport as early as possible in order to land at Djakarta well in time.

After landing at Hong Kong, all the crew members went through Immigration and Customs and complied with the requisite formalities. Captain Jatar, Co-Pilot Dikshit and Flight Navigator Pathak went over to the Operations Office of Air India International at the airport to complete the Flight Plan and then to the Meteorological Office (MET Office) at the airport to get a briefing on weather forecast and general weather conditions en-route from Hong Kong to Djakarta. From the MET Office they went to the Air Traffic Control to obtain the clearance for take-off. After completing these tasks, the three of them proceeded to the airport restaurant for lunch.

In the meantime, a transit check of The *Kashmir Princess* was carried out by the Hong Kong Air Craft Engineering Corporation, under the supervision of the plane's Maintenance Engineer, Karnik, who had joined as a member of the plane's crew on the afternoon of April 10, at Bombay Airport. Refuelling was also carried out. Thereafter, the luggage was loaded and the passengers (i.e. the advance party of the Chinese delegation) also boarded the plane and took their seats. The Kashmir Princess was at Hong Kong Air Port for about 80 minutes. Carrying the advance party of the Chinese Delegation, she took off at about 1326 hours (Hong Kong Time) on Monday, April 11. She passed east of Indo-China, keeping close to the coast. The flight was routed to fly over the Great Natuna Islands which are an integral part of Indonesian territory. The plane was flying normally. The Flight Navigator Pathak got a pin-point at North Natuna Island and was looking over for further islands of the Natuna group. After having

Disaster in the Air : The Crash of the Kashmir Princess   23

reached the northern islands of the Natuna group he gave a position report at about 1715 hours (local time) to Singapore and Djakarta. In the meantime, the Air Traffic Control (ATC) at Djakarta airport made a query as to whether the Chinese Premier was on board the aircraft, to which a reply in the negative was given.

The *Kashmir Princess* was at that time cruising at an altitude of about 18,000 feet when the cockpit crew detected a fire in the luggage compartment. Immediately, she issued a distress signal, called MAYDAY - at about 1730 hours (local time) stating "fire in the luggage compartment". The signal was picked up clearly by the Air Traffic Control (ATC) of Djakarta airport.

The Djakarta ATC called The Kashmir Princess thrice and when there was no response from her, they relayed messages on radio to all air ports in the vicinity to the effect that distress signal MAYDAY had been heard thrice from the aircraft. The Djakarta ATC received a message from the Singapore ATC indicating the position of The Kashmir Princess which was somewhere near the Natuna Islands. The Djakarta ATC immediately passed on the information to the Indonesian Air Force Headquarters (AURI) and also to the Djakarta headquarters of Garuda Indonesian Airways.

The Singapore ATC informed the Djakarta ATC that one Sunderland Aircraft and one speed boat had been sent out to locate the plane. At about 2100 hours (local time) on April 11, the Djakarta ATC received a message from one of the planes of Qantas Australian Airlines which was at that time flying from Bombay to Calcutta, that it had heard about an aircraft having crashed somewhere near Natuna Islands.

Immediately after receipt of the distress signal from The Kashmir Princess, the Singapore ATC had alerted the RAF Search and Rescue Organisation. The estimated position of The Kashmir Princess at the time of her distress call, was calculated and passed on by the RAF Controller to be within ten miles of the crash position to the Rescue Control Centre (R.C.C.). The R.C.C. agreed late in the evening on April 11, to two Indonesian Air Force planes joining the search along with the RAF Sunderland aircraft.

At about 1900 hours (Djakarta time) on April I l, Mr. Tyabji, informed me that The Kashmir Princess, carrying the advance party of the Chinese Delegation, had sent MAYDAY distress signal while flying over Singapore region. These MAYDAY signals had been received by the Djakarta ATC at about 1755 hours (Djakarta time) on April 1 l. The Indian Ambassador asked me to get in touch with the Headquarters of the Indonesian Air force immediately and to ascertain further details regarding the fate of The Kashmir Princess and to get back to him as early as possible.

I immediately got in touch with the Chief of the Indonesian Air Force, Air Marshal Suryadarma. He informed me that he had already alerted the Air Force which was taking necessary action, even though the exact location of the crash of The Kashmir Princess into the sea had not yet been determined. However, the position of the aircraft at the time of its crash into the sea was computed later and was found to be in the region of the group of islands called the Great Natuna Islands which were within the territorial waters of Indonesia.

The Angatan Udara Republic of Indonesia (AURI) i.e. the Indonesian Air Force, deployed a Dakota with night take-off capability from Halim airfield (Djakarta) in order to reach the Natuna Islands at day-break the following day, April 12. At the same time, a Catalina flying boat was also alerted to take off at first light on April 12 in order to reach the Natuna Islands in the vicinity of which The Kashmir Princess was reported to have crashed. Thus, these two planes of the Indonesian Air Force joined the RAF Sunderland Aircraft late in the evening on April 11 for search operations.

On the morning on April 12, the chief of the Indonesian Air Force called me to his office and informed me that the site of the crash of The Kashmir Princess had been identified as being in the vicinity of the Natuna Islands. He gave me the following additional information :

- A message had been received from the Singapore ATC to the effect that the RAF and the Civil Aviation had confirmed that the islanders in the small islands of the Natuna group had seen a burning plane crash into the sea on the afternoon on April 11.
- The authorities in Singapore further mentioned that the first message of sighting the wreckage of the ill-fated Kashmir Princess had been received from m.v."Taype", a 250-ton cargo boat, while sailing in the direction of the crash and that the burning plane had plunged into the sea near the Djack and Batu Billis Islands of the Natuna group, roughly 250 miles north-east of Singapore.
- The Taype, a cargo ship plying under the British flag, had for over 35 years been operating a regular service between Singapore and the Natuna group of islands. The port of Genting on the island of Sedanau in the Natuna group of islands, was a regular port of call for the cargo ship. The Taype had arrived at the port of Genting at 0635 hours on April 12.
- The islanders of Sedanau Island living near the port of Genting had

- also reported having picked up some pieces of luggage.
- On receipt of the message from the Taype, an RAF Sunderland flying boat had been directed to proceed towards the site of the crash.
- In addition, one high-speed RAF launch and the British frigate H.M.S. Dampier had been directed to proceed towards the site of the crash.
- Three survivors had been picked up by the villagers of the island near the site of the crash.
- The AURI Dakota had reached the site of the crash and had begun conducting an air search to locate other survivors, if any.

I called on Ambassador Tyabji immediately and conveyed to him all the information gathered by me from the Chief of the Indonesian Air Force. The Ambassador communicated the information immediately on wireless to the Afro-Asian Joint Secretariat and to the Ministry of External Affairs, New Delhi.

As the air crash had taken place in the territorial waters of Indonesia, the Civil Aviation Department of Indonesia took immediate action, in consultation with their Foreign Office, to constitute a Commission of Inquiry to investigate into he crash of The *Kashmir Princess*.

The news broadcast from Radio Peking, monitored at Djakarta on April 12, 1955, charged the Governments of the United States of America and of Nationalist China (i.e. Formosa) had deliberately engineered the crash of The Kashmir Princess in a plot to kill the Chinese Premier, Mr. Chou en-Lai, and the Chinese Delegation to the first Afro-Asian Conference which was scheduled to be held in Bandung on Monday April 18. The news broadcast further added that the British Government must also bear the responsibility for the crash, since The Kashmir Princess had taken off from Hong Kong, which was at that time under British Administration, stating : "We demand that the British Government and the British Authorities in Hong Kong should conduct a thorough investigation into this incident and arrest and punish, according to law, the secret agents taking part in this sinister plot"

Indonesian newspapers mentioned that before The *Kashmir Princess* took off from Hong Kong on April 1 1, the Government of the People's Republic of China had got information that there was a plot to harass and molest the members of the Chinese delegation, who were at that time in Hong Kong, either on their way to the Hong Kong airport or at the airport itself. The Chinese Government had officially brought the above intelligence report to the notice of the British Charge d'Affaires in Peking on April 10, requesting him to alert the authorities concerned in Hong Kong.

The Indian Premier Mr. Nehru was reported to have stated in New Delhi : " This disaster has some very unusual features. Ten minutes before the Aircraft fell into the sea, we had a normal message from it. Something must have happened suddenly soon after. There will be a full enquiry into all this ". The Government of India sent a telegram to the Chinese Premier Mr. Chou en-Lai, expressing deep regret over the crash and promised to make full investigation.

A spokesman of the British Foreign Office in London, obviously taking a serious view of the charges made by the Chinese Government, was reported to have stated : " We await full report and must withhold comment until then. We do not like commenting on something very important like this until we have the full story."

The State Department of the U.S.Government was reported to have stated that the allegations and insinuations made by the Chinese Government were "preposterous", since the aircraft (Kashmir Princess)which was in Hong Kong airport for about 80 minutes in the forenoon on April 11, 1955, was "ringed" with security guards.

The Minister of Communication of Indonesia, called on the Indian Ambassador in Djakarta in the forenoon on April 12, requesting him to nominate a senior and suitable officer of the Indian Embassy to accompany the Commission of inquiry constituted by the Government of Indonesia to investigate into the crash of The *Kashmir Princess*. After consulting the Ministry of External Affairs, Govt. of India, New Delhi, the Indian Ambassador in Djakarta, Mr. Tyabji, nominated me to represent India on the Commission of inquiry constituted by the Govt. of Indonesia. At a press conference held in the evening on April 12, in Djakarta, Mr. Tyabji stated that an Indonesian Air Force plane carrying the members of the Commission of inquiry constituted by the Govt. of Indonesia to investigate into the causes of the crash of The *Kashmir Princess* (including Col. A.K..Mitra, Military, Naval and Air Attache in the Indian Embassy in Djakarta as the accredited representative of the Government of India) will be shortly proceeding to the Natuna Islands for on-the-spot investigations. He further disclosed that at about 1745 hours (local time) on April 11, 1955, an "All Okay" message had, in fact, been received from The Kashmir Princess by the Air Traffic Control (ATC) of Djakarta Air Port - that is, about ten minutes before the ill-fated *Kashmir Princess* plunged into the sea in the vicinity of Natuna Islands.

Meanwhile, I had been meeting various people in Djakarta and the Indian members of the Joint Secretariat of the Afro-Asian Conference to gather as much information as possible about the air crash, particularly in view of the allegations made by the Chinese Government and rejoinders

Disaster in the Air : The Crash of the Kashmir Princess 27

issued by the British and the U.S. Governments . Frankly, I found the entire situation to be confusing since I had no information or knowledge of the real facts of the story. I wondered whether there had indeed been a plot to kill the Chinese Premier and the members of the Chinese Delegation and thus sabotage the first Afro-Asian Conference. I had almost no knowledge of the characteristics and technical details of commercial aircraft such as the Lockheed Constellation of U.S.Make. 1 had some knowledge of military aircraft of Allied and enemy forces of World War-II, having attended courses at the Royal Air Force Station at Amman (Transjordan) in 1942 and later at the Royal Air Force Training Establishment in the U.K. during 1946-1947.

Mr. Alan Chaves, formerly of Air India International and at that time an Aviation Instructor in the Indonesia Air Academy, Djakarta, on deputation from the International Civil Aviation Organisation, based in Canada, was a very trusted friend. I felt that if I could manage to have him appointed as an adviser to the Commission of inquiry, the entire Commission would benefit from his technical knowledge, advice and guidance.

On April 13, during a meeting with Dr. Sugato, Director General of the Indonesian civil aviation organisation to discuss the constitution of the Commission of inquiry, I suggested that, having regard to his qualifications, experience and background knowledge of civil aviation organisations and their functioning, Mr. Alan Chaves may be co-opted as Technical Adviser to the Commission of Inquiry. My suggestion was unanimously accepted by all the members of the Commission including the Indonesian Director General of Civil Aviation. Mr. Alan Chaves was co-opted to assist the Indonesian Government as Technical Adviser. The other members of the Commission were : Mr. R.J.Imawan, Air Traffic Control Section, Indonesia; Engineer Soetomo, Technical Department, Civil Aviation, Indonesia, Engineer J.Heyligers. Airworthy Section, Civil Aviation; and Dr. M. S. Kamminga, Operations Manager, Garuda Indonesian Airways, Djakarta.

Dr. Sugato announced that the Commission of Inquiry would leave early morning on Thursday April 14, 1955 by an Indonesian Air Force plane for Pontianak on way to the Natuna Islands, to make on-the-spot enquiries and investigations on Friday April 15, 1955, very close to the scene of the disaster.

ANNEXURE - 6

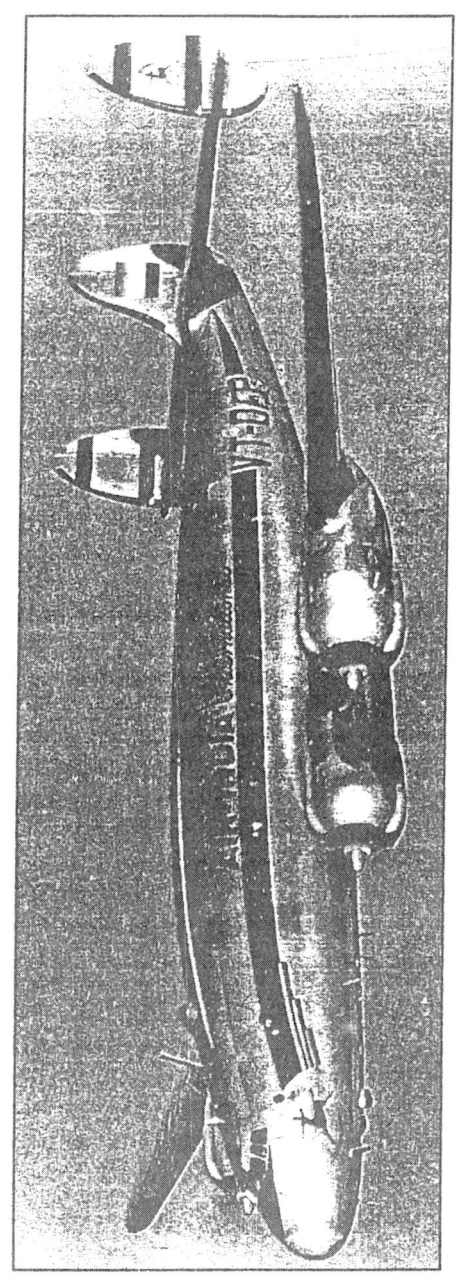

'Kashmir Princess'

Disaster in the Air : The Crash of the Kashmir Princess

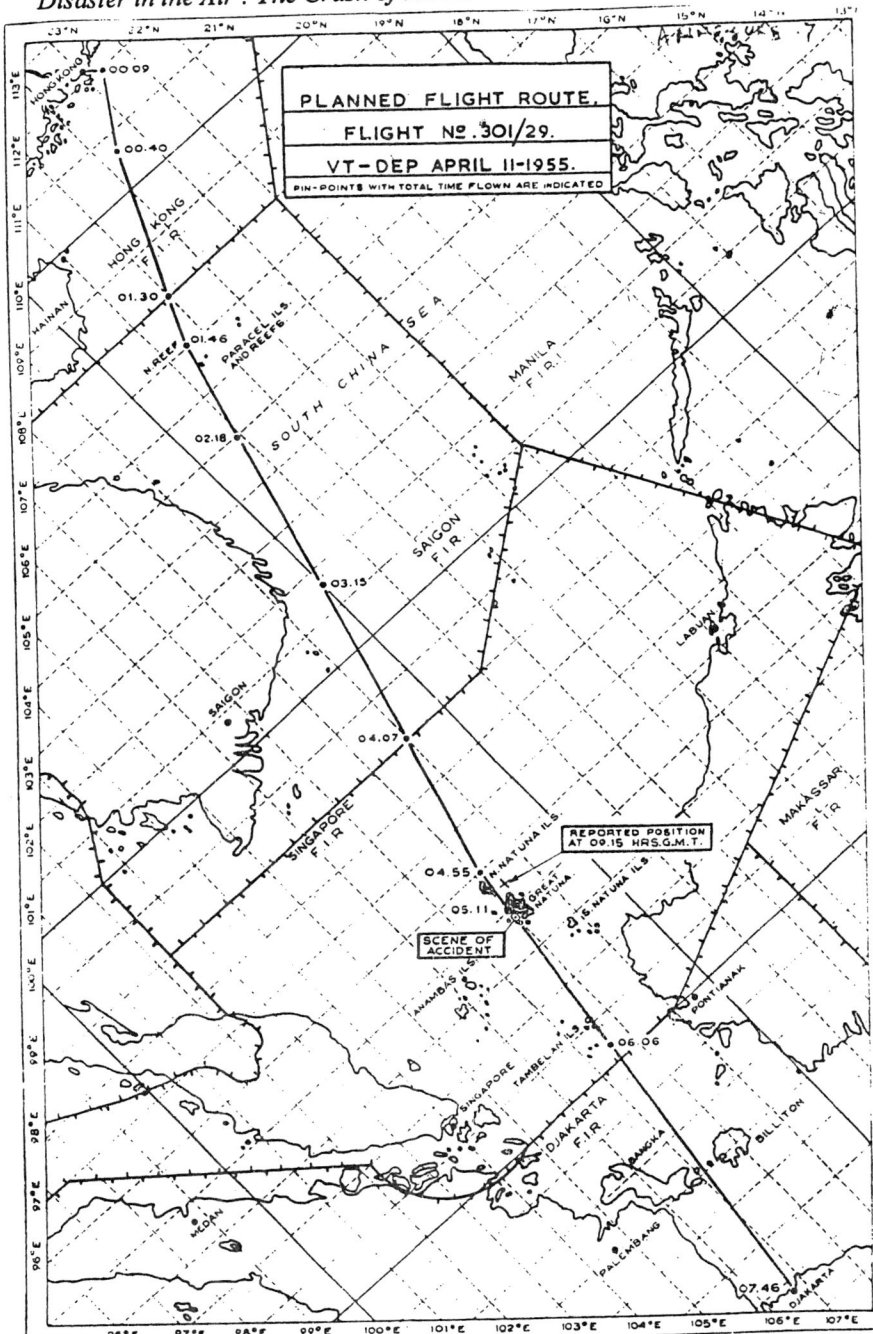

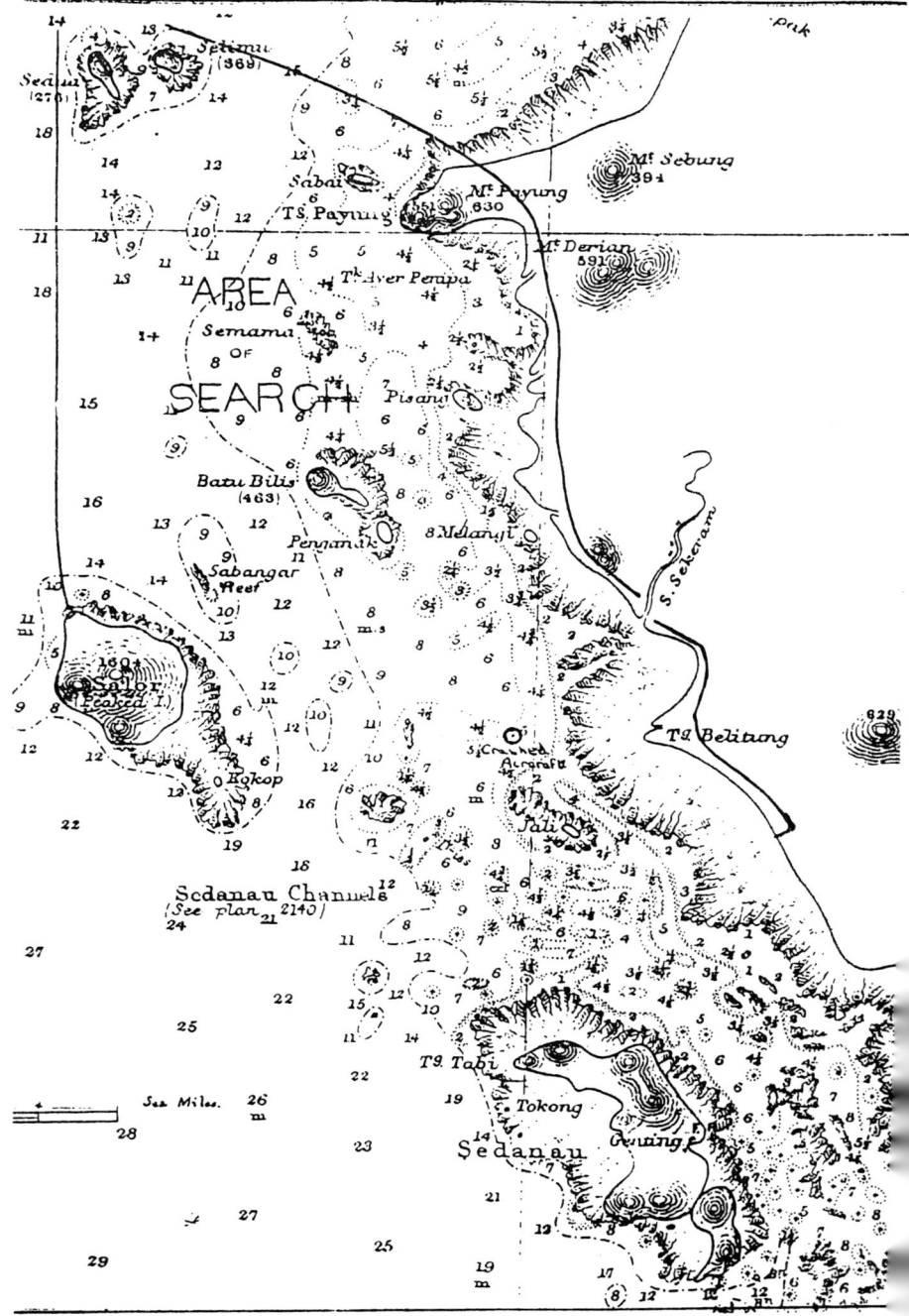

Chapter 5

INQUIRY COMMISSION INTERVIEWS EYEWITNESSES

The members of the Commission of inquiry including myself and Mr. Alan Chaves (an Indian national) boarded an Indonesian Air Force (A.U.R.I.) Dakota aircraft at Halim Air Force base (Djakarta) at 0600 hours in the morning on April 14, to proceed to Pontianak en route to Natuna Islands. All of us were in a state of high excitement.

Our aircraft landed at the Indonesian Air Force Base at Pontianak at about 1500 hours on April 14 and we stayed overnight at Pontianak. Early the next day, Friday April 15, at about 0700 hours, we boarded the Air Force flying boat "Catalina" which prepared to touch down at about 1200 hours in shallow seas in the vicinity of Sedanau Island. The five-hour flight in the Catalina was a veritable ordeal on account of the cold. Mr. Alan Chaves and myself huddled together to keep ourselves warm. We could see very little of the outside through the small round glass windows.

As the Catalina was about to touch down in sea water, the pilot noticed, just in the nick of time, that there was a huge coral reef at the point of landing. The pilot quickly steered the Catalina away to a safer stretch of the sea, thereby averting a disaster. All of us on board the Catalina expressed our appreciation of the pilot's alertness and presence of mind.

We proceeded to Genting, a small sea port on Sedanau Island, where we were received by the Indonesian Naval and Air Force officials. A large number of villagers were eagerly awaiting our arrival. Some of these villagers were eye-witnesses to the crash of The Kashmir Princess and they were all agog with excitement to narrate to the Commission what they had seen between 1745 hours and 1800 hours (local time) on the evening on April 11, 1955. The Chairman of the Commission kindly translated to me the eye-witness accounts of the villagers.

Those who had actually seen a burning plane plunging into the sea off Sedanau Island and had spotted and picked up the three survivors, (namely Co-Pilot M.C. Dixit, Maintenance Engineer A.S.Karnik and Flight Navigator J.C.Pathak) had taken them in motor boats to Sedanau Island

(Genting) and placed them in the custody of the local authorities at Genting, The Commission recorded their statements. The three crucial eye witnesses, all from Great Natuna, were :

1. Musa, 18 years of age, a farmer from Pulau Bunguran Barat;
2. Wan Saban, 50 years of age, a farmer firom Pulau Batu Bilis;
3. Madjun, 40 years of age, a copra trader from Pulau Bunguran Barat.

The gist of the statement made by Musa was as follows :

"On the afternoon on April 11, 1955, as I was paddling my praw (boat) in the sea I saw an aircraft coming from the direction of Semama Island which was in between Batu Bilis Island and Salor Island. I saw clearly that the whole aircraft was on fire and black smoke was coming out of its fuselage and further that the aircraft was descending rapidly and then plunged into the water, making a shallow dive. For the short period I saw the aircraft in flight, I noticed that the noise coming from the rapidly descending aircraft was quite unusual. I was not however able to see the aircraft actually hitting the water as the entire aircraft was covered in dense black smoke and it was at a distance of three miles from the praw which I was paddling, I however remembered the spot where the aircraft hit the water and immediately, I paddled to Kuala, the nearest island, where I borrowed an outboard motor which I fitted in my praw and then sailed back towards the site of the crash, taking four people with me. According to my recollection, the time was between 1745 hours and 1800 hours. As the sea was calm 1 was able to reach the site of the crash at about 1930 hours. I remembered having seen a lifejacket with an electric light, reddish in colour , and yellow colour below it.

When the Inquiry Commission showed to him a life jacket, he said that he had seen an inflated life jacket on which several items were found. He picked up books, six small cushions, an empty bag, three pieces of wood and three uninflated lifejackets. While he did not see any burning oil on the surface of the sea water, his hands became dirty because of oil having got mixed with sea water. He did not hear any sound and was not able to say how deep the sea was at the site of the crash.

He carried the things picked up by him to Genting and handed them over to the officials of the local Administration. At the request of the Administrator, on the following day (that is, April 12) he escorted the Administrator accompanied by two policemen to the spot where he had picked up the articles. Even after circling the area for some time, they could not find anything else.

That night at about 9 p.m., he saw an aircraft with search lights

Disaster in the Air : The Crash of the Kashmir Princess 1955 33

but it was flying far away from the site of the crash.

The gist of the statement made by Wan Saban was as follows :
At about 5.30 p.m. in the afternoon on April 11, 1955, while he was working in his field in Batu Bilis Island, he heard some unusual sounds of an aircraft. On looking up, he saw an aircraft to the north-west, the tail and fuselage of which were on fire and black smoke was coming out from the aircraft in spasms. He saw the aircraft descending rapidly and then hitting the water. The aircraft appeared to slide over the water for a few seconds. As the aircraft was on fire and was covered in dense black smoke, he was not able to see things clearly. When the smoke disappeared, he saw neither the aircraft nor anything else on the surface of the water.

On account of the low tide, it was not practical for him to take out his praw and paddle towards the site of the crash and therefore he went home. At about 7 p. m., he heard the sound of a motor boat. He rushed to the shore from where he saw a flashlight at the spot where the aircraft had plunged into the sea. Then he saw another motor boat coming towards the spot on the shore where he was standing. He met Said from Ajer Nali alongwith 12 men in the motor boat. He got instructions to remain on the island and to keep a watch. At about 10 p.m. at night, he saw an aircraft circling over the spot where the aircraft had plunged into the sea and dropping red and green flares.

Early morning on the following day he sent out two of his men to the shore to keep a watch. At that time, the two men spotted two survivors of the crash. The two survivors were found wearing life jackets over their uniforms and one of them had a small beard. The two survivors were taken to the house of Wan Saban. He got two boats ready to take them to Genting in Sedanau Island and to hand them over to the local authorities. One of the survivors was found to be walking with difficulty and he was taken aboard the boat with great care.

When the boat carrying the two survivors as well as the other boat had left the shore of the island , another survivor was spotted waving to them from a nearby island. The two boats were rowed to that island and the third survivor was also taken on the same boat which was carrying the other two survivors. The third survivor was also found wearing a life jacket over his striped shirt and a bandage on his left arm. He was able to walk easily. As the two boats (one of them carrying the three survivors) were proceeding towards Genting, four aircraft were seen hovering in the air above them. The three survivors tried their best to draw the attention of the crew in the four aircraft by waving their life jackets but in vain. The two boats reached Genting (in Sedanau Island) where Wan Saban reported to the police alongwith the three survivors.

The gist of the statement of Madjun was as follows :
"Early morning at about 5.30 a m - 6 a m on April 12, I saw two men on Batu Bilis Island sleeping under a tree. He immediately rushed to call Wan Saban. When he returned with Sabau, he found that one of the men had got up. Both men were found wearing lifejackets over their uniforms and one of them had a small beard." The local doctor and the clergyman also gave their version.

The Captain of the cargo ship "Taype" which was sailing in those waters in the evening on April 11, 1955, was also an eye-witness of the crash of The *Kashmir Princess*. The villagers who had actually picked up the three survivors took them in motor boats to Sedanau Island (Genting) where the "Taype" took the survivors on board. Later, the three survivors were transferred to H.M. S Dampier, a British naval ship, which proceeded to Singapore so that the three survivors could get proper medical attention and treatment without delay. The members of the Commission recorded the statements of all the eye-witnesses of Sedanau Island who had come to Genting.

At Genting (Sedanau Island), the members of the Commission saw the body of one of the victims of the crash of The *Kashmir Princess* (Flight Purser C.d'Souza) which had been cleaned and enveloped in white tissue as the body was in an advanced stage of decomposition and had been kept in the local polyclinic. As per instructions received from the authorities of the local church, the Commission arranged for the cremation of the body of Flight Purser C.d'Souza.

The members of the Commission saw some salvage recovered from the ill-fated *Kashmir Princess* which was later kept in the custody of the Indonesian Naval Police Headquarters. The wreckage of The *Kashmir Princess* had actually settled on a shallow coral reef, even though the depth of the sea, in high tide, near the scene of the crash was about 30 feet, (that is, about five fathoms).

The members of the Commission stayed at Genting overnight and took off for Djakarta the next day, April 16, at about 1400 hours in an Indonesian Air Force Heron aircraft which landed at about 1700 hours (local time) at Kamajoran airport, Djakarta.

The Air India Constellation, carrying the Indian Prime Minister Mr. Nehru, the President of Egypt, Mr. Gamal Abdel Nasser, the Prime Minister of Burma, U Nu, the Foreign Minister of India, Mr. V.K.Krishna Menon and several senior members of the delegations of the respective countries, had arrived at the Kamajoran Airport, Djakarta, a little earlier

Disaster in the Air : The Crash of the Kashmir Princess 1955   35

than the Indonesian Air Force Heron aircraft carrying the members of the Inquiry Commission.

After disembarking from the aircraft, as I was walking towards the airport terminal building, the Indian Ambassador Mr. Tyabji came out followed Mr. Nehru. I was stopped short of the terminal building. The Prime Minister, worry and anxiety writ large on his face, took me aside and enquired as to what had actually happened to The *Kashmir Princess* that it should have crashed into the sea all of a sudden. I briefed our Prime Minister about the work done by the Inquiry Commission till that time and conveyed to him what we had heard from eye-witnesses and what we had seen at Genting (Sedanau Island) the previous day, April 15. I further informed Mr. Nehru that the Commission would be interviewing the three survivors of the crash who were reported to be undergoing medical treatment at Singapore, in order to ascertain the actual cause of the mishap. Thereafter, the Commission would make arrangements to salvage the wreckage of The *Kashmir Princess* from the sea as it had reportedly settled on a shallow coral reef. Noticing that I looked very tired and exhausted and that my uniform was dirty and smelly, the Prime Minister said that he would like to meet me later after I had had some rest. He introduced me to the President of Egypt, Mr. Gamal Abdel Nasser, the Prime Minister of Burma, U Nu, India's Foreign Minister, Mr. VK.Krishna Menon and other dignitaries who were present there.

Chapter 6

WHAT THE SURVIVORS HAD TO SAY

As I was about to drive home from the airport, the Chairman of the Commission, Mr. Imawan, informed me that the Director General of Civil Aviation Mr. Sugoto, would like to meet the members of the Commission at his office at 1900 hours that evening (April 16) to discuss and finalise the further programme of work of the Commission and to apprise the Commission of the latest information received by him from various sources. The members of the Commission attended the conference in Mr. Sugoto's Office at 1900 hours. During the meeting, we were informed that the three survivors of the crash had left Singapore and had already reached Bombay from where they would be proceeding to their respective homes. It was decided that the Commission must leave for Bombay the very next day, Sunday April 17, in the early morning. It was felt that the members of the Commission must fly non-stop from Djakarta to Bombay in order to reach Bombay in time and for this purpose a suitable aircraft was required. Dr. Sugoto and the other members of the Commission agreed to my suggestion that I should approach the Indian Prime Minister Mr. Nehru with the request to allow us to take the Air India Constellation aircraft (which had brought him and other dignitaries to Djakarta earlier that day - April 16, 1955) to Bombay early morning the next day (April 17) with the assurance that the aircraft would be sent back from Bombay to Djakarta immediately after dropping the members of the Commission at Bombay. Dr. Sugoto and the other members of the Commission said that they would wait till my return from the residence of the Indian Ambassador Mr. Tyabji.

When I conveyed the Commission's request, Mr. Nehru readily agreed to place the aircraft at the disposal of the Commission for the day. The favourable response of the Prime Minster was indicative of his sincere and deep concern and anxiety for the speedy conduct and progress of the investigations by the Commission. The Prime Minister added that the Chinese Premier Mr. Chou en-Lai had brought to his notice the intelligence reports from Hong Kong regarding the sabotage to The *Kashmir Princess* at Hong Kong airport on April 11. Mr. Nehru cautioned me that the information given by the Chinese Premier must be kept strictly confidential at that stage and that I should guide the Commission accordingly. After thanking the Indian Prime Minster for his kindly gesture, I returned to Dr. Sugoto's office and gave them the good news that the Indian Prime Minister had allowed the Commission to take the Air India Constellation to Bombay the following morning. It was decided that all the members of the Commission should assemble at Kamajoran Airport at 0600 hours on April 17 and that the Air India Constellation should take off at 0730 hours for Bombay. It was further decided that Dr. Sugoto would inform the Air India authorities in Bombay and the Indonesian Consul in Bombay to make necessary arrangements for our reception at Bombay airport and for accommodation in Bombay for the members of the Commission for the duration of their stay.

Our aircraft took off from Kamajoran airport at 0730 hours on April 17 and after a long and tiring flight of 11 hours, landed at 1830 hours at Santa Cruz Airport, Bombay. The members of the Commission were received by senior officials of Air India International Corporation and by the officials of the Indonesian Consulate in Bombay. Accommodation had been arranged in the Taj Mahal Hotel, Bombay.

The Commission felt that it might take one full day to get complete information about the organization of Air India International, the functions of various departments and other technical aspects from the officers of Air India. Accordingly, the Commission decided to meet senior officials of Air India at its office at 1000 hours on April 18. It was further decided to meet two of the survivors of the crash, Co-Pilot M.C.Dikshit and Maintenance Engineer A.S.Karnik, at their residences on the morning on Tuesday April 19, 1955. The third survivor, Flight Navigator J.C.Pathak, had already left Bombay for his home in Calcutta.

On the morning on April 18, 1955, before going to the Air India office, I called up my old friend Lt. Col. Butalia, G. S.O.I Bombay area. I also spoke on the trunkline to Brigadier D.Choudhury, Director of Intelligence, Army Headquarters, New Delhi, and informed him of my arrival in Bombay as a member of the Inquiry Commission.

While the members of the Commission were in discussion with the officials of Air India, Mr. Kaw, a senior officer of the Intelligence Bureau, arrived from New Delhi and wanted to join the discussions. However, his request was turned down by the Chairman of the Commission. Thereupon, Mr. Kaw gratefully accepted my suggestion that he should come to the Taj Mahal Hotel in the evening where I would brief him about all that had transpired between April 11 and April 18. Mr. Kaw informed me in confidence that he was on his way to Peking to liaise with the Chinese authorities in their investigations regarding the crash of The Kashmir

Princess. He suggested that I get in touch with him later in case he could be of any assistance to the Inquiry Commission. On the evening on April 18, 1955, the Commission had a meeting in the office of the Indonesian Consulate in Bombay to discuss future plans.

At about 1000 hours on the morning on Tuesday April 19, the members of the Commission visited the flat of one of the three survivors, Co-Pilot Captain M.C.Dikshit, with flowers and a box of sweets. At first Capt Dikshit refused to meet us, the Commission, presumably under the mistaken impression that the inquiry was being conducted on behalf of Air India. However, I managed to enter the flat and got into the drawing room where I saw Capt Dikshit sitting on a chair. I explained to him that our Commission had been constituted by the Government of Indonesia. I informed him that the Indian Prime Minister had readily agreed to spare the Air India Constellation aircraft to enable the members of the Commission to reach Bombay well in time to meet the survivors of the crash. The Prime Minister was anxious about the health of the survivors and to know the cause of the crash of The *Kashmir Princess*. Furthermore, I informed Capt Dikshit that the Commission would be calling on Maintenance Engineer Karnik the same day and then fly on Wednesday April 20, to Calcutta to meet Flight Navigator J.C.Pathak.

After hearing my explanation, Capt Dikshit appeared to regain his composure and heartily welcomed the other members of the Commission into his drawing room. He looked very tired and was obviously in severe pain having suffered multiple abrasions and fracture of the right clavicle at the time of the crash of The *Kashmir Princess*. His arm was in a sling.

After the members of the Commission were introduced to Captain Dikshit, he expressed his profound gratitude to the Government of Indonesia and to the people of Sedanau Island (Indonesia) for having done all that was possible for him and for his other two surviving colleagues. He said that the people in Sedanau Island in general did more than other agencies of the Government of Indonesia. Even little children had come forward to help the three survivors. He added that the Captain and the crew of the cargo ship Taype and of the British frigate *HMS Dampier* were equally helpful as they had given first aid and medical treatment to the three survivors and had made them comfortable while on board their ships.

The oral statements made by Capt Dikshit for more than three hours were taken down in short hand. Some of the members of the Commission also made notes individually even as Capt. Dikshit was narrating the events and incidents of April 11, 1955.

The Commission adopted the same procedure while interviewing and interrogating Aircraft Maintenance Engineer Karnik at his residence the same afternoon and Flight Navigator Pathak at Dum Dum Airport, Calcutta on April 20.

After giving a brief account of the interview with each of the three survivors, I shall present, later in this narrative, a combined account of the statements made by them, in order to avoid repetition.

At about 1730 hours in the evening the same day the members of the Commission visited the residence of the Aircraft Maintenance Engineer A.S.Karnik to take down his statement.

After the members of the Commission were introduced and after the usual exchange of greetings, Karnik began to narrate the facts and circumstances until the time of the crash. He stated that he was throughout inside the aircraft at the Hong Kong airport except for about ten minutes when he had gone to the toilet in the terminal building. When he returned to the aircraft, he found that all the passengers had already boarded the aircraft and had occupied their seats. Initially, he took his seat in the tourist compartment of the aircraft. About five minutes after take-off he moved over to the crew compartment and sat there for the next hour. At that time, he observed that all the critical and vital sections of the aircraft were in perfect working order. Thereafter, he returned to the tourist compartment of the aircraft where he took his seat in the second row in the rear on the left hand side of the aircraft and fell asleep.

At the time of the crash, he was braced over the table in the Navigator's compartment and sustained moderate injuries. He suffered multiple abrasions, laceration in the occipital region and fracture of the proximal phalanx of the right little toe.

After the crash, the three survivors had been spotted by some of the islanders of Sedanau Island and had been brought to the small port town of Genting on the Island where their injuries and wounds had been dressed provisionally and thereafter, the three survivors had been initially taken on board the cargo ship *Taype* from where they had been transferred to the British frigate *Dampier*. On board the *Dampier*, the three survivors had been examined by the ship's Medical Officer, allowed Karnik to move after making sure that there was minimal weight bearing on the right foot. The *Darmpier* arrived on April 14, at the Port of Singapore whence the three survivors had been sent to the Royal Naval Sick Quarters H.M.S.Terror for further medical treatment.

Karnik also expressed his profound gratitude for the hospitality and kindness shown by the islanders of Sedanau Island who had rescued the three survivors and brought them to Genting. Karnik recalled that one of the islanders, obviously a good dresser, had dressed his wounds very well. He added that as soon as he got well and was fit to travel, he would once again visit Genting to thank the islanders and also the Captain and crew of the *Taype* and the British frigate *Dampier* for all that they had done for him.

The statements made by Karnik during the three-hour interview of the Commission with him were taken down in short-hand.

Later in the evening of the same day, Alan Chaves and I visited the residence of the victim of the crash, Captain D.K.Jatar, to express our heartfelt condolences to his wife Mrs. Jatar. Later, we visited the residence of the mother of Mrs. d'Souza, where the young wife of another victim of the crash Flight Purser C.d'Souza was also present.

Though Mrs. Jatar was in a state of shock, she maintained her composure and said that she was deeply touched by our visit. She said that she had sent several telegrams to Prime Minister Nehru at Bandung, appealing to him to use his influence to have a thorough search undertaken to trace her husband as she believed that her husband was still alive and was perhaps wandering about in one of the uninhabited islands of Natuna. We assured her that the Government of Indonesia and the Indian authorities were doing everything possible to search for other survivors of the crash.

Alan Chaves and I felt very sad on meeting the young wife of the victim of the crash, Flight Purser C.d'Souza. We expressed our heartfelt condolences to her. She appeared to be somewhat relieved when we informed her that Alan Chaves and I had personally organised and supervised the last rites of her husband with the help of the authorities of the local church in Genting (Sedanau Island) and that his remains had been interred in the compound of the church on April 16.

The members of the Commission left Bombay for Calcutta by an Indian Airlines Skymaster, which took off from the Santa Cruz Airport, at about 1430 hours on Wednesday April 20 and after a three-hour flight, landed at Dum Dum Airport, Calcutta, at about 1530 hours the same day. The Commission interviewed *in camera* at Dum Dum Airport the last of the three survivors, Flight Navigator J. C. Pathak, the same night.

The 28 year old Flight Navigator J.C.Pathak had, as a result of the crash, sustained multiple abrasions, with burns on the face and fracture of the left radius and ulna with displacement. His left hand had been plastered. As a result of the prompt medical treatment, he was much better and looked quite fit. Accompanied by his elder brother, a senior Railway officer, Flight Navigator J.C.Pathak had arrived at Dum Dum Airport a few minutes before the arrival of the members of the Commission.

After an exchange of greetings with the members of the Commission and offcials of Air India International who had accompanied the members of the Commission, Flight Navigator J.C.Pathak started narrating the events and incidents which had taken place on April 10, 1955 at Bangkok and on April 11, at Hong Kong Airport and on the flight of The *Kashmir Princess* from Hong Kong towards Djakarta on April 11, 1955. He said that after landing at Hong Kong, Capt Jatar, Capt Dikshit and himself completed all their official duties and then went to the airport restaurant for their lunch.

While the three of them were having their lunch, a person who introduced himself as a journalist came to their table and enquired as to when the Chinese Delegation was expected to arrive and as to the duration of the flight from Hong Kong to Djakarta. He was told that they had no information as to when the Chinese Delegation would arrive and that the duration of the flight from Hong Kong to Djakarta would be about seven hours and forty-five minutes. At this point, in reply to a query by the Commission as to whether the stranger was a Chinese national, the Flight Navigator J.C.Pathak stated that while he was not sure about the nationality of the stranger, he was not a Chinese nor an Indian. Going by the features and complexion, the stranger appeared to be either an European or an American. The Flight Navigator J.C.Pathak added that the three of them did not think much about the incident nor did they take any notice of the stranger and did not ask him any questions.

The Commission recalled that while taking down the statement of Capt Dikshit at his flat in Bombay on April 19, he had also mentioned that while they were having lunch in the airport restaurant in Hong Kong Airport, a young American gentleman had walked in and had taken a seat at their table. Capt Dikshit did not like the American taking a seat at their table, without knowing who he was. The stranger had addressed his queries to Capt Jatar and sometimes to Capt Dikshit and J.C.Pathak. In reply to his query as to when the plane was expected to leave, he was told that the plane would take off in about an hour's time. In reply to his query as to how long the plane would take to reach Djakarta, he was told that the plane was expected to land in Djakarta at night. The three of them did not like to give any details to the stranger. Capt Dikshit had said that he disliked the stranger from the very beginning since he had not introduced himself properly. In fact, the stranger had made himself objectionable by his general behavior. The three of them never thought about the stranger afterwards.

During the interrogation of the Flight Navigator J.C.Pathak at Dum Dum Airport, he mentioned that while they were going back to the aircraft after lunch, Capt Jatar had mentioned to them on the way that he had heard rumours that some local people were trying to create trouble for the members of the advance party of the Chinese Delegation to the first Afro-

Asian Conference and therefore the authorities in Hong Kong were going to take some precautionary measures.

During the interrogation of the Aircraft Maintenance Engineer A.S.Karnik at his Bombay residence the previous evening, he had mentioned that while he was carrying out checks on The *Kashmir Princess*, at Hong Kong airport on April 11, Mr Bombaywale, Operations Officer of Air India at Hong Kong Airport, had told him to be alert and to be on the look-out for strangers, if any, who may be found loitering about around the aircraft. The Aircraft Maintenance Engineer Karnik had told him that since he was himself a stranger in Hong Kong, he could not possibly know who was a stranger and who was not and further it was the duty of the Police and Airport Security to apprehend strangers and suspicious-looking characters, who may be found within the premises of Hong Kong Airport.

The members of the Commission stayed overnight on April 20 at the Airport Guest House in Dum Dum Airport. Several representatives of the Press had gathered there and had requested to be briefed about the progress of the investigations by the Commission and their findings till that point of time. The Chairman of the Commission, Mr. R.J.Imawan, requested me to meet and brief the representatives of the Press regarding the terms of reference of the Commission and how the Commission would be carrying out their investigations.

Addressing the representatives of the Press; I informed them that the most important task of the Commission was to salvage the wreckage of the aircraft. This was a difficult task and would necessarily take time. Therefore, there may be some delay in the submission of the Commission's Report to the Government of Indonesia. Once the wreckage of the aircraft had been salvaged from the sea and was subjected to a thorough technical examination, it would go a long way towards determining the cause of the accident. I further informed the representatives of the Press that the members of the Commission had visited the site of the crash and had made necessary arrangements for the salvage of the wreckage. The actual salvage operation would be carried out in the presence of the Commission. To facilitate the investigation, Mr. G.Appuswamy, Chief Technical Adviser to the Chairman of Air India International, would also accompany the Commission. Two ships of the Indonesian Navy had been positioned at the site of the crash to guard the wreckage. There were small islands in the vicinity of the crash which were inhabited but had no facilities for transport. Search and rescue operations were continuing near the site of the crash in order to locate other survivors, if any, and the bodies of the other victims of the crash.

I informed the representatives of the Press that the Commission had, on 18th and 19th April, recorded the statements of Mr. Bombaywale, Operations Officer in the office of Air India at Hong Kong airport (he was available in the Head Office of Air India International at Bombay on April 18) Co-Pilot Capt M.C.Dikshit and Aircraft Maintenance Engineer, A.S.Karnik. The members of the Commission had also met Mrs. Jatar, wife of Capt D.K.Jatar, commander of the aircraft and Mrs. d'Souza, wife of Flight Purser C.d'Souza whose body had been cremated in Genting, and had conveyed their condolences to them. The Commission had recorded the statement of Flight Navigator J.C.Pathak earlier in the evening. At Singapore, the Commission proposed to record the statements of the Chief Officer of the cargo ship *Taype* and the Captain of the frigate *H.M.S.Dampier*, which were involved in the initial rescue operations on l2th, 13th and 14th April. The Commission would be spending one day at Singapore. Thereafter, the Commission would split into two groups, one group would proceed to Hong Kong to record the statements of the authorities in Hong Kong airport such as Airport Security and Airport Police. The Commission might also record the statement of Mr. K.M.Raha, Deputy Director General, Civil Aviation, Government of India, who had already conducted a departmental investigation at Hong Kong airport. The members of the Commission would return to Djakarta by April 22.

The Consul General of Indonesia and other officials of Calcutta Airport were present at Dum Dum Airport when the members of the Commission left Calcutta at 0230 hours on Thursday April 21, by an aircraft of the British Overseas Airways Corporation (BOAC) which landed at 1230 hours (local time) the same day at Singapore.

At Singapore, the Commission planned to record the statements of a total of twenty-seven persons who were connected with the flight of The Kashmir Princess and subsequent rescue operations after its crash into the sea, keeping in view the following aspects :

A. Circumstances at Hong Kong airport in general, prior to the take-off of The *Kashmir Princess*.
B. Communication and Air Traffic Control (ATC) proceedings in Singapore Flying Information Region (FIR) Organisation.
C. Search and Rescue operations initiated in Singapore FIR.
D. Communication and Air Traffic Control proceedings in Djakarta FIR Organisation.
E. Search and rescue operations in Djakarta FIR.

The *Kashmir Princess* was flying over Singapore FIR when it transmitted MAYDAY distress calls over the wireless. These signals were received at about 1725 hours (local time) on April 11, by Radio Station Kamajoran (Djakarta) which, in turn, relayed the distress signal to the ATC at Singapore Airport.

I have mentioned earlier that, in order to avoid repetition, I would present in a consolidated manner the statements of the three surviving members of the crew of the ill-fated *Kashmir Princess*, who had been interviewed by the Commission in Bombay on April 19 and in Calcutta on April 20. Accordingly, the events, incidents and circumstances as nanated by the three smvivors are presented below in chronological sequence :

The crew members of The *Kashmir Princess* on its flight firom Hong Kong to Djakarta were the same as that which had flown the aircraft from Bangkok to Hong Kong under the command of Capt Jatar. After its arrival at Hong Kong airport, the plane was at the airport for about 80 minutes. During this period, a transit check of the aircraft was carried out by Hong Kong Aircraft Engineering Corporation under the supervision of Aircraft Maintenance Engineer Karnik. After refuelling, involving an intake of 2,520 imperial gallons of fuel, the aircraft was carrying a total of 3,780 imperial gallons of fuel and 140 impetial gallons of oil. The crew members received necessary briefing on the route and flight plan and on weather conditions.

The aircraft had on board eleven passengers consisting of eight oflicials of the Govemment of the People's Republic of China, two journalists from Poland and one official of the Government of North Vietnam. The Chinese offcials constituted the advance party of the Chinese Delegation to the Afro-Asian Conference scheduled to take place at Bandung (Indonesia) on April 18. The luggages of the passengers had been loaded into the aircraft.

On receipt of clearance for take-off from the Air Traflic Control of Hong Kong Airport, The *Kashmir Princess* took off at about 1326 hours (Hong Kong time) on April 1 1. Capt Jatar was in connmunication with the Hong Kong control tower. The aircraft was flying over the south-west gap and then changed over to approach frequency and again contacted Hong Kong control tower on long range to pass on the departure message which Flight Navigator Pathak had given to the Co-Pilot Capt Dikshit. The aircraft avoided all Chinese islands and passed east of the coast of Indo-China, slightly west of the track, to keep close to the coast.

Every now and then Capt Jatar enquired from Dikshit whether the aircraft was clear of the Chinese islands. Dikshit informed him that the aircraft was far away from the islands. Capt Dikshit and Flight Navigator

Pathak were watching through the window on either side of the aircraft. Capt Jatar took the aircraft to the cruising altitude of 18,000 feet and after it had levelled out, Dikshit engaged the automatic pilot. All the while, both normal and operational messages were passed by the aircraft over the wireless to the Air Traffic Controls of airports enroute.

In the meantime, Pathak charted the pin-point at North Natuna Island and was looking for the other islands of the Natuna Group. Dikshit got up from his seat, went to the rear, lay down and dozed off. On the track marked on the chart, Dikshit had seen, prior to the take-off, a group of coral islands; and one of these islands bore the name "Bombay Island". Dikshit had never seen a coral island and he was curious to see Bombay Island because of the "Bombay" in its name. He woke up after a little while and asked for the position. Pathak informed him that the plane was in fact flying over those coral islands. Dikshit came forward and looked through the window to have a good look at the coral islands. Thereafter, he went back into the galley and was talking to the Flight Pursers C.D.'Souza and J.J.Primento. The pursers informed him that no passenger had asked for any liquor, perhaps because the passengers were not the drinking type. The pursers added that most of the passengers had a youthful appearance but then it was difficult to judge the age of the Chinese as they all looked young. They appeared to be busy reading newspapers. There was hardly any conversation between the passengers and the crew. After having a cup of tea, Capt Dikshit went back to his Co-Pilot's seat.

Both Capt Jatar and Capt Dikshit were relaxed and cheerful throughout the flight. Inspite of the long flight, they were not tired. After some time, Jatar went into the cabin, leaving Dikshit in the Co-Pilot's seat.

As the aircraft was flying over Saigon flying information region (FIR) Dikshit sent a position report to the Saigon Air Traffic Control (ATC) and after about half an hour, he again contacted Saigon ATC to inform them that the flight was normal at that time. Dikshit had presumed that it was the Saigon ATC which informed him that the position last reported by the aircraft was wrong. Since that seemed odd to Dikshit, he asked Pathak to recheck their last position. Pathak checked up and informed Dikshit that their report on the last position of the aircraft was in order. Dikshit thereupon called up Saigon ATC again to inform them that their last position report was correct. (He later recalled that it was not the Saigon ATC but the Singapore ATC which had challenged their position, since the aircraft was at that time flying over Singapore FIR and not Saigon FIR). On the basis of Dikshit's last message that their last position report was correct, if the Saigon ATC had passed on that message to the Singapore ATC, it was obvious that the Singapore ATC was in fact also plotting the flight of The *Kashmir Princess*.

When Jatar returned to the cockpit, Dikshit informed him about the communications with the Saigon ATC and the Singapore ATC. Jatar enquired why the Singapore ATC was plotting the aircraft's position on a chart (since it was not normally done). Dikshit commented that the Singapore ATC was perhaps under the impression that it was an important flight and therefore they were making doubly sure and plotting the flight. When the aircraft passed over from the Saigon FIR to the Singapore FIR, a weather forecast was obtained from the latter. At that time The *Kashmir Princess* was cruising above the clouds at an altitude of 18,000 feet. Jatar asked Dikshit to request Singapore ATC to inform Djakarta ATC that The *Kashmir Princess* would require night-landing facilities at Kamajoran Airport, Djakarta. Promptly acknowledging the message, the Singapore ATC also confirmed that the message had been passed on to Djakarta Airport. Radio communication between the aircraft and the Saigon ATC and Singapore ATC was excellent.

It was at about 1715 hours (Singapore time) that Dikshit transmitted the aircraft's last position to Singapore ATC. Thereafter, a wireless message was received by the aircraft from Djakarta, which was quite clear, enquiring whether the Chinese Premier, Mr.Chou en-Lai was on board the aircraft, to which a prompt reply was given by the aircraft in the negative. At that time, that is about 1715 hours (Singapore time), when the aircraft was flying over the northern part of the Great Natuna Islands, Flight Navigator Pathak gave a position report to Singapore as well as to Djakarta.

At about 1720 hours (Singapore time), as Pathak was standing in the Flight Navigator's compartment, he heard the sound of an explosion. The nature of the sound produced by the explosion was similar to the sound heard when the under-carriage of an aircraft goes up and locks after take-off. It was not a loud sound but was more like the sound of a thud. Co-Pilot Dikshit also heard it at the same time. The explosion had shaken the whole aircraft. Aircraft Maintenance Engineer Karnik was awakened from his sleep by the noise of the explosion - he felt that the noise was similar to the sound produced when a heavy load was dropped on the floor of a cabin. He immediately got up to look around and to find out what had happened. Karnik also remembered what Mr. Bombaywale (Manager, Operations Office of Air India International at Hong Kong Airport) had cautioned him about at Hong Kong airport in the forenoon of that very day, that is, to be on the look-out for strangers and suspicious looking characters who may be found loitering about around the aircraft, since the passengers in that tlight were communists and there was a possibility of sabotage.

Whether some heavy object had really dropped on the cabin floor or he was just imagining things, Karnik rushed to the crew compartment to enquire whether any of the other crew members had heard that noise. At that moment, Karnik noticed that smoke was coming into the cabin from the individual cold-air outlets provided in the aircraft. He immediately rushed to the cockpit and informed Capt Jatar that, in all probability, there was an outbreak of fire in the rear luggage compartment of the aircraft. Since both Capt Jatar and Capt Dikshit appeared to be unperturbed, Karnik felt that the outbreak of fire was probably in the rear luggage compartment since the front luggage compartment was below the cockpit and his own seat was just above the rear luggage compartment.

Pathak was trying to investigate the cause of the explosion at the same time. He also noticed that smoke was coming into the cockpit. At that point, when everyone on board the aircraft was trying to find out the cause of the explosion and the smoke, one of the cabin attendants reported that the right wing of the aircraft was on fire. The fire was very near the fuselage on the trailing edge of the wing. Immediately Pathak looked out through the window and saw that the right wing of the aircraft had indeed caught fire.

Dikshit felt that the sound produced by the explosion had been louder than that of a thud and it had shaken the whole aircraft. He also saw the smoke, somewhat whitish in colour, coming into the cockpit, where he was occupying the co-pilot's seat alongside that of the pilot, Capt Jatar. Dikshit had no idea where the noise had come from but he surmised that it had most probably come from the rear and from below the cabin floor.

Karnik rushed to the cockpit when Dikshit enquired where the smoke was coming from, since he apprehended that the electrical system of the aircraft might soon be on fire. Flight Engineer K.F.D. Cunha immediately switched off the generators. When Karnik observed that, in his opinion, the fire had broken out in the luggage compartment in the rear under the cabin floor, the electrical system was again switched on.

Capt Jatar ordered flight engineer D'Cunha to explode one set of the fire extinguisher bottles in the luggage compartment in the rear. Dikshit sought instructions from Capt Jatar whether he should immediately transmit over the wireless the MAYDAY signal to the Singapore and Djakarta ATC. Meanwhile, D'Cunha and Karnik put the sound trap lever to "off" position and discharged one set of the fire extinguisher bottles into the luggage compartment in the rear. At that moment, Pathak came into the cockpit and reported to Capt Jatar and Dikshit that the right wing of the aircraft had caught fire. Karnik immediately rushed back to the cabin to ascertain the

Disaster in the Air : The Crash of the Kashmir Princess 1955

exact location of the fire. He found out that fire had broken out between no. 3 and no. 4 engines near the trailing edge. At that moment looking out of the cabin window, Karnik's assessment was that the fire was not very dangerous and it may die out on its own. Karnik again looked through the viewing lenses and also by opening the hatch, to find out whether there was any outbreak of fire in the front luggage compartment and was, however, relieved to find that there was none. Thereafter, he rushed back to the cockpit and informed Capt Jatar about the location of the fire on the right wing. Karnik returned to the cabin to keep a watch over the fire and found, to his horror, that the fire was spreading very rapidly and noticed yellow and red flames emanating from that part of the wing. Karnik rushed back to the cockpit and informed Jatar that, having regard to the serious nature of the fire on the right wing of the aircraft, it was his considered view that Capt Jatar must ditch the aircraft as soon as possible.

At that very moment, Flight Engineer D'Cunha reported to Jatar that the hydraulic system of the aircraft had failed. In the presence of Dikshit, Karnik and D'Cunha who were all in the cockpit at that time, Jatar exclaimed "they have done us". In view of the gravity of the situation, Jatar took over control of the aircraft manually. When Dikshit heard D'Cunha reporting to Jatar that the hydraulic system had failed, he immediately switched "ON" the auxiboosters. When Jatar observed that the controls appeared to be O.K. Dikshit informed him that the controls appeared to be functioning normally because he had switched "ON" auxiboosters. Dikshit switched off the auxiboosters to make Jatar realise that the controls were functioning on auxiboosters and then switched "ON" the auxiboosters again. (The auxibooster is an independent system for operation of the controls of an aircraft. In the event of the failure of the hydraulic system, the auxiboosters are provided as a stand-by. This system is independent and is located near the controls. The controls respond through the movement of the control columns).

The *Kashmir Princess* was at that time flying at an altitude of 18,000 feet. Karnik came back to the cabin to observe the extent of the fire. Again, to his horror, Karnik found that the fire had intensified and was fast approaching the wing root end of the aircraft. He again rushed back to the cockpit and reported to Capt Jatar that the right wing of the aircraft may, in all probability, disintegrate and drop off on account of the fire, within the next few minutes and that, he felt it imperative to "ditch" the aircraft immediately.

Dikshit again asked Jatar whether he should send the MAYDAY signal (the signal of extreme distress) by wireless to the Singapore ATC and the Djakarta ATC. Jatar said that he wanted to be more definite before agreeing to a MAYDAY signal. Jatar was throughout in his seat in the cockpit and Dikshit was holding on to the controls as best he could. The fire warning light appeared on the "master fire warning" on the instrument panel in the cockpit in front of the pilot, Capt Jatar. Dikshit noticed on the instrument panel that the fire warning light had pointed to no.3 engine on the right wing of the aircraft. As ordered by Jatar, one set of fire extinguisher bottles had been exploded by Flight Engineer D'Cunha sometime earlier in the luggage compartment at the rear. Smoke continued to come into the cockpit and Jatar ordered D'Cunha to explode another set of fire extinguisher bottles into the luggage compartment. Flight Engineer D'Cunha reported that that set of frre extinguisher bottles on board was the last set. Jatar shot back "Never mind. Explode it". Flight Engineer D'Cunha exploded the last set of the fire extinguisher bottles into the luggage compartment in the rear. Immediately thereafter, the fire warning light which had appeared on the instrument panel in the cockpit in front of Capt Jatar's seat went "OFF ".

It was then that Jatar asked Dikshit to send the MAYDAY signal. Dikshit complied immediately and also gave the aircraft call sign. He sent MAYDAY signals again and again giving the aircraft's call sign two or three times to the Singapore as well as to the Djakarta ATC. He again repeated the MAYDAY signal adding "fire in the luggage compartment". He wanted to add the word "sabotage" to the message but did not do so while actually sending the MAYDAY signal.

Meantime, Karnik carried three life jackets for handing over to the three members of the crew in the cockpit, since he could not carry five life jackets at the same time, the two additional life jackets being intended for Flight Engineer D'Cunha and himself. He saw that the air hostess was already carrying two life jackets and was helping the Pilot and the Co-Pilot to put them on, while Karnik helped Flight Engineer D'Cunha to put his life jacket on.

Thrusting the life jacket into Capt Dikshit's lap, the air hostess, Miss Gloria Berry, asked him to wear it. When she found that Dikshit was not making any effort to put on his life jacket because both his hands were busy with the controls of the aircraft, she loudly appealed to him to wear the life jacket. Dikshit took the life jacket from his lap and put it around his neck and left it there. The air hostess and the two pursers provided life jackets to all the eleven passengers who were sitting quietly and calmly in their seats.

The *Kashmir Princess,* which was flying above the clouds at an altitude of 18,000 feet, was rapidly losing height and was descending. Flight Navigator Pathak was aware that the aircraft was going to be ditched

Disaster in the Air : The Crash of the Kashmir Princess 1955   51

and he was therefore trying to be on watch to find out the position where the aircraft would eventually ditch. He kept Dikshit informed of the position. Jatar and Dikshit were both busy trying to maintain the trim of the aircraft and to keep it "on level". When Dikshit picked up the mike of the radio system to send radio message to Singapore and Djakarta ATCs to convey the position of the aircraft, he found that the aircraft's radio telephone had "packed up" . Pathak overheard the conversation between Jatar and Dikshit from which he gathered that since there was no hydraulic pressure available, they would be trying to make a flapless landing perhaps on the surface of the water.

During that time, Karnik was busy opening the emergency exits of the aircraft as instructed by the captain of the aircraft. He opened the first emergency exit on the port side over the left wing of the aircraft and then the emergency exit in the Flight Navigator's compartment. When these two emergency exits were opened, he found that dense black smoke had filled the cabin and the cockpit, and he was unable to move further to open other emergency exits or the cabin door. Karnik was in the Flight Navigator's compartment and he was about to collapse due to suffocation but suddenly some fresh air came into the Navigator's cabin. He took one deep breath and looked out of the emergency exit and found that the water was just about 3 or 4 feet below the aircraft. He knew it was impossible to do anything further before the aircraft actually touched the water and the next instant, he found that he was under water.

In the cockpit, since Capt Jatar could not control the aircraft all by himself, he asked Capt Dikshit to help him to maintain the trim of the aircraft and to keep it on level. Full left rudder was on, Capt Jatar pressing on it. Full left aileron was also on but Capt Jatar was finding it extremely difficult to control the aircraft. Capt Dikshit helped him with the trim and with the controls, leaning over his side. When dense black smoke started filling the cockpit, Capt Jatar could not even see the instrument panel in front of his seat, so he opened the storm window in front of his seat. A blast of cold air came in, clearing the air and enabling Capt Jatar and Capt Dikshit to see where the aircraft was going. Karnik was aware that it was impossible to do anything further before the aircraft actually hit the surface of sea water. He folded his hands on the Flight Navigator's table and rested his head over his hands. Realising that the aircraft was about to ditch, Pathak sat down on the front seat in the Navigator's compartment and braced against the bulkhead for ditching.

The decision to ditch was finally taken by Capt Jatar when Karnik shouted "You must ditch". Capt Jatar replied "We are ditching". Capt Dikshit pointed out to Capt Jatar a particular island which was not marked on the map. Capt Jatar said that the island was too near and was not suitable, turning to port at the same time, and said that the aircraft would be ditched there in the shallows. Capt Dikshit accepted the decision of Capt Jatar.

As the aircraft was descending fast, Capt Dikshit noted that the speed of the aircraft was about 215 knots or thereabouts. The altimeter which had, sometime earlier, indicated the altitude as 10,200 feet, was now indicating the altitude as 2,000 feet, further dropping to 1,800 feet. The aircraft was still on fire. Capt Jatar and Capt Dikshit did not have full control over the flight of the aircraft notwithstanding "full left aileron and rudder". The right wing was too low. Capt Dikshit picked up the mike of the radio system and shouted "Hello ! Hello!" into it but there was no life in the radio system.

Right from the time that Karnik reported to Capt Jatar and Capt Dikshit about the explosion and outbreak of fire in the luggage compartment under the cabin floor in the rear of the aircraft, Capt Jatar had kept his cool and did not panic. He was in the habit of speaking slowly. When he said in a calm and steady voice to Capt Dikshit :"open the storm window", Flight Engineer D'Cunha shouted to Capt Dikshit : "Open it Dicky". Dikshit opened the storm window, taking off his hands from the control columns, just about one third, fearing that immediately after ditching, sea water might gush into the cabin with full force. Thereafter, Dikshit quickly brought his hands back on the control columns. As the Co-Pilot. it was his responsibility to ensure that the final operation of "ditching" was carried out in a proper manner. As the cockpit was still filled with dense black smoke, he was not able to see Capt Jatar.

The aircraft came down very low. Capts Jatar and Dikshit found that the aircraft was still considerably "nose down". Dikshit pulled the stick back and the aircraft balanced a little. He then felt the forward pressure on the stick obviously exerted by Capt Jatar to prevent the aircraft from gaining height again. He bent down to see the speed of the aircraft, as he felt that the time for ditching was imminent. He gave a shout when he saw on the instrument panel that the speed of the aircraft had declined to 140 knots. It was then a question of further loss of speed of the aircraft. When D'Cunha shouted to Capt Dikshit "Ditch it quick, the right wing will fall off", Dikshit had no time to look back and held on to his seat.

After a little while, when the aircraft was flying very close to the surface of the sea, the starboard wing (that is, the right wing) of the aircraft touched the water. He was not quite sure if the starboard wing had broken off. The next moment, the aircraft ditched. Dikshit presumed that the starboard wing had disintegrated and had fallen off into the water,

Disaster in the Air : The Crash of the Kashmir Princess 1955

since the aircraft went down as soon as it hit the surface. He estimated that the aircraft had hit the surface of sea water at a flat angle, almost level.

It was absolutely dark inside the cockpit as it was still filled with dense black smoke. Dikshit noticed that the cockpit was now full of water. He realised that so much water could not have come into the cockpit through the partially opened storm window and surmised that water must have come in through the emergency exits which had been opened or due to breakage of the fuselage. He unstrapped himself and groped for the sliding window, as he thought that the sliding window was the only means of escape. With all the strength at his command, Dikshit pushed the sliding window open and pushed his body through but it became jammed and his feet were without support. He somehow managed to get a foothold and then he managed to inflate his life jacket. By this time, his lungs were bursting and he would not have been unable to hold his breath even for half a minute more. He started kicking at the foothold he had found a little earlier and suddenly, felt released. He started floating up to the surface. He was perhaps at a depth of about 30 feet and while shooting up towards the surface, he had swallowed some sea water. He was able to breathe as soon as he surfaced. As he was floating on the surface with his life jacket on, he saw several objects from the aircraft floating about on the surface. He saw a large object which he surmised to be the port wing of the aircraft which had just sunk into the water. He also saw some objects on fire and a lot of smoke.

With one hand he grabbed a plywood plank measuring about 2½ feet square which was floating on the surface near him. He rested his arm on the plank and remained still in order to avoid being hurt by the fire which was close to him. A considerable amount of oil from the wing of the aircraft had leaked out and was burning in patches on the surface and some of these patches were only about two or three feet away from him. At that moment, he heard Karnik shouting at him "get away from the fire". With the plywood plank in hand, he paddled himself and was soon drifting away from the fire when he spotted Karnik. He discarded the plywood plank as he found it too cumbersome.

At the time the aircraft ditched, Karnik was in the Flight Navigator's compartment. As the aircraft sank, he found that he was under water. He managed to come to the surface and saw a wall of fire about 20 feet behind him. He also saw the port wing of the aircraft sticking out through the fire, with the wing tip pointing towards the sky. He noticed that a portion of the cabin, which had apparently broken off, was floating about 10 feet ahead of him. He swam towards it and climbed on it. He saw Pathak and Dikshit coming out of the water. Pathak was close to the fire on the surface. He kept on shouting at Pathak to get away from the fire. Then he shouted at Dikshit asking him to join him so that all the three of them could swim together towards land.

When the aircraft had ditched, Pathak had been sitting in the Flight Navigator's compartment. As the aircraft went down, Pathak found himself deep down in the water. He struggled to come up to the surface and it took him half a minute or so to do so. He was a good swimmer. When he was floating on the surface of the water with his life jacket on, he saw a big fire almost next to him. Pathak inflated his life jacket and was trying to get away from the fire. At that moment, he spotted Karnik quite away from the fire and he heard Karnik shouting at him "Come away". He shouted back at Karnik telling him that he was finding it extremely difficult to move away from the fire. While he was trying hard to get away from the fire, it seemed that the fire was overtaking him. If the fire had not died down of its own, Pathak might have got badly burnt. He started swimming towards Karnik when he discovered that his left fore-arm was broken. He then spotted Karnik and Dikshit not very far from the spot where he himself was floating. Pathak also heard a voice shouting in pain. He shouted back "Come here". Twice the voice asked where Pathak was. Thereafter, Pathak did not hear anything from the "voice" - and did not know who he was. Pathak surmised that the man who was shouting was perhaps the Flight Engineer D'Cunha but was not sure.

Besides the three of them (that is Dikshit, Karnik and Pathak) Karnik saw two persons floating on the surface of the water and heard one of them, in a clear voice with Indian accent, shouting at them "where are you". By that time, the three of them had gone a considerable distance away from the spot where the two men were seen and were unable to return to that spot.

Dikshit, Karnik and Pathak were swimming together. Everything was quiet all around. The three of them looked around and sighted a small island close by. Dikshit suggested that they should move towards another island which was not much farther and which had a longer coast line and that island might be a better proposition in the event the three of them drifted apart. Karnik and Pathak readily agreed with Dikshit's suggestion and then all the three of them started swimming together. Being a better swimmer, Pathak was going a bit fast but kept looking back at the other two. Dikshit and Karnik asked Pathak to go ahead and told him that they would follow him.

When the three of them were swimming towards the larger island, the local time (Singapore time) was about 1800 hours. They kept blowing their whistles from time to time to keep in contact with each other. Being a good swimmer, Pathak had a considerable lead over the other two. After about two hours of swimming, it became quite dark and the three of them could not see each other. Pathak, who was swimming faster towards the larger island, soon got separated from the other two. At that moment, Pathak saw two torches flashing in his direction and in response, he flashed his torch.

Since Pathak was swimming faster, he was far ahead of Dikshit and Karnik who were unable to see him or hear his voice or whistle. The two of them blew their whistles once or twice to draw Pathak's attention but it was no use. With his broken collar bone, Dikshit was finding it extremely difficult and painful to swim using his right hand as a paddle. He also noticed that his life jacket was leaking and he took the mouth piece and blew it in order to re-inflate the life jacket. Karnik also blew into his life jacket to re-inflate it as his life jacket also had sprung a leak. Even after more than two hours of swimming, they were nowhere near the coast of the larger island.

Earlier, soon after sunset (about 1815 hours Singapore time), the three of them had seen from their respective positions on the surface of the water, an aircraft flying overhead with lots of red lights on its belly and dropping parachute flares. One of these flares dropped very close to the spot where Dikshit and Karnik were floating and lit up the area on the surface of the water surrounding the two. Presumably, the aircraft had already heard of the crash of The *Kashmir Princess* and was perhaps looking for survivors of the crash but failed to spot the three survivors floating on the surface of the water even though the lights on their life jackets were lit. The aircraft was about 2000 feet above the surface of the water, almost directly above Pathak, who was flashing his torch at the aircraft. The aircraft must have failed to spot Pathak who thereafter kept on swimming towards the larger island.

In the meantime, Dikshit and Karnik saw at a distance of about a mile a powerful beam of light directed towards them. They presumed that someone was coming to rescue them. Another torch light also flashed in their direction. A little later, however, both the torches went off. Being in a very happy mood that someone had spotted them, Dikshit told Karnik that he expected that someone would be coming in a boat to pick them up in a few minutes' time. However, there was no sign of any boat or anyone coming towards them. By that time, the three of them had been swimming for almost five hours.

Suddenly, a storm blew up and it started raining. As the clouds were low, the three of them were not able to see anything in front of them. Dikshit and Karnik tied themselves with the tape from their life jackets to avoid drifting apart and then continued to swim together. When the storm died down and the rain ceased and the clouds cleared a bit, they found themselves in a different part of the open sea. They saw an island close by but they found they were swimming against the current. By then they had been afloat and swimming for about eight hours. Suddenly Karnik hit a rock and then both of them had to make their way over the corals. It was a strenuous task for them to reach the land. They were spotted and rescued by the inhabitants of the island on the morning of the following day, that is, April 12.

When the weather cleared up, Pathak continued swimming towards the larger island. After swimming for about half an hour, Pathak found that he was swimming against the current. He made a rough guess as to the direction of the current and started swimming with the current, leading to another island. After swimming for about ninety minutes, he hit some coral reef and soon found that he was almost on the island. He walked to the shore and then he badly wanted to take some rest and get some sleep but could not do so, due to the cold breeze blowing over the island. He decided to take a brisk walk to keep himself warm and also to find out if people were living on that small island. Having covered the island, he went to sleep and woke up in the morning of the following day, that is, April 12. He then took another round of the island and in the process came across a hut; but there was no one inside. The hut gave him some hope that people were living on that island. He sat down near the hut. He somehow bandaged his fractured fore-arm and used his neck-tie as a sling. He then got up and took yet another round of that small island, when he saw another island nearby where some canoes had been lined up. He started whistling and waved his life jacket. After about five minutes, he saw two canoes coming towards him. When the first canoe reached the shore of the island, he saw two familiar faces in the second canoe which was following. They were Capt Dikshit and Karnik. He felt immense relief on seeing his two colleagues and with great excitement, Pathak joined them in the same boat.

When the three survivors were re-united, the time was about 0900 hours of April 12. Pathak learnt that the two boats would be taking them to the nearest village which was on Sedanau Island located about ten miles away and that it would take about five hours to reach that island where they would be given medical attention. It spoke volumes for the humanity, kindness and thoughtfulness of the boatmen that they carried food and tea and bedding for the three survivors. The boatmen gave them water and then some snacks followed by hot tea.

The wrist watches of the three survivors were still showing Hong

Kong time and it was about 0900 hours (Hong Kong time) of April 12 when the two boats started on their journey. After about an hour, they saw three flying boats (Sunderland aircraft) flying low overhead. The three survivors hoped to catch the attention of the men in the aircraft by waving their life jackets. They presumed that the aircraft crew had spotted them when the three aircraft again flew low over them. The three survivors once again waved their life jackets to catch the attention of the aircraft crew. They, in fact, saw a man looking out of the window from the fuselage, located aft of the wing. They were almost sure that the crew of the three aircraft had spotted them and were hoping that the aircraft would land nearby. However, the three aircraft kept on hovering over the area without making any effort to land. Everytime the aircraft flew over them, the three of them waved their life jackets. They were doing this for almost two hours before they gave up. (When the Investigation Commission interviewed Karnik at his residence in Bombay on Tuesday April 19 Karnik had said that, the Captain of the cargo ship Taype told him that the Sunderland aircraft of the Royal Air Force of the U.K. had informed him by wireless that the Government of Indonesia did not grant permission to the Sunderland aircraft landing in Indonesian waters).

The two boats took about five hours to reach their destination, the small port of Genting on Sedanau Island. On arrival, the three survivors were warmly welcomed by the people of Genting. Apart from food, the three of them were given pillows, bed sheets and other comforts. There was a medical attendant in Genting and he was as good as a doctor. He dressed the wounds and fractures of the three survivors and did everything that could be done.

At Genting, an officer from the cargo ship *Taype* told them that all arrangements had been made to take them on board. He brought the Chief Officer of the ship. Capt Dikshit dictated to him the following message which was at once transmitted to Singapore : "Three survivors have been picked up and there are three more possible survivors". The Chief Officer of the Taype informed them that he was in communication with the Sunderland aircraft of the Royal Air Force. They were still searching all over the coast. The survivors wondered why any permission was at all required when the Sunderland aircraft were genuinely engaged in search and rescue operations to locate and then to rescue the survivors of the air crash. If the Royal Air Force could not get prior permission of the Indonesian Government to land in the territorial waters of Indonesia there was no point deploying the Sunderland aircraft (flying boats) for rescue purposes!

The Chief Officer of the *Taype* informed the three survivors that the ship would be navigated out of the territorial waters of Indonesia and then transferred to *H.M.S. Dampier,* a ship of the Royal Navy, which would be coming from Singapore and waiting outside Indoneisan waters. The *Dampier* had on board adequate medical facilities including a well-equipped dispensary. The Chief Officer of the *Taype* also mentioned that he had in fact met the Medical Officer of the *Dampier* and had suggested to him that the survivors be moved on stretchers. After spending about two hours at Genting, the three survivors were taken on board the Taype whose Captain, Chief Officer and stewards were very kind to them. Since the survivors were not in a very bad shape, they were able to board the ship on their own and once they were on board, the ship's doctor took every care of them.

The *Taype* crossed Indonesian waters and entered Malaysian waters, where the *Dampier* was waiting to take the three survivors to Singapore. The three survivors were transferred to the *Dampier.* On its way to Singapore, the ship received a radio message from the base to the effect that the ship should go around the site of the crash in search of other survivors. The captain decided to anchor the ship for the night of April 12/13 and to carry out further search operations during daylight hours next day. After reaching the site of the crash, the ship's divers went down into the water and were able to locate the wreckage of the aircraft which had apparently been spotted earlier by the Sunderland aircraft. Three bodies were recovered by the divers and from the papers found on them, two bodies could be identified by the ship's crew as that of Flight Engineer D'Cunha and Flight Purser Primenta. The identity of the third body could not be established.

A diver informed Dikshit that the wreckage of the aircraft was found lying at a depth of about 32 feet and that nobody was found in the cockpit. While there was no damage on the inside of the cockpit, the nose cap of the aircraft was flat or "gone inside". In reply to Dikshit's query, the diver said that he had not seen any window open. He added that he had only seen the window screens with the wipers intact and further that it would require one more day to look into the cabin since the visibility was very poor.

The captain of the *Dampier* informed Dikshit that an Indonesian ship would be coming to carry out further search and diving operations and therefore the *Dampier* would go back to its base at Singapore. The Captain asked Dikshit whether the ship should carry the three bodies to Singapore or hand them over to the Indonesian ship which was expected at that spot. Dikshit replied that it would be necessary for him to contact the head office of Air India International at Bombay, as the question of taking care of the three bodies was an important matter. The Captain decided

Disaster in the Air : The Crash of the Kashmir Princess 1955

to take the three bodies on board and then proceed to Singapore.

On the morning of the following day (April 13), the three survivors were listening to the radio in their "sick" room, when they heard the Government of the People's Republic of China making allegations regarding the crash of The *Kashmir Princess*. Dikshit advised Karnik and Pathak that since the accident had taken such a political turn, it would be better for them not to say anything to anybody except to the Inquiry Commission which was the official body (constituted by the Government of Indonesia) entitled to have first hand information. From the ship, they sent messages to their families in Bombay and Calcutta that they were well.

On reaching Singapore on April 13, the three survivors met the Admiral of the British Fleet at Singapore, Indian High Commissioner in Malaya, Mr. R.K.Tandon, Mr. R.N.Kaul, General Manager, Air India International, Singapore and Mr. Vishwanath, an officer in the Bombay Office of Air India International. The three survivors stayed at the Singapore Naval Sick Bay *(H.M.S. Terror)* for two nights. From there, they were shifted to Singapore General Hospital where they had to stay for a day. All three of them desired that arrangements should be made immediately for their flight from Singapore to Bombay. Accordingly, Air India International, Singapore, made arrangements for their flight from Singapore to Bombay early morning on April 17, 1955 but at 0655 hours, they were informed that they were required. to stay back since the Inquiry Commission was expected to arrive at Singapore on that very day to interview them. However, Mr. R.K.Tandon, Indian High Commissioner in Malaya and Mr. Vishwanath of Air India International, Bombay, felt that it might cause a great deal of inconvenience to the three survivors and a great deal of anxiety to their families if they were not allowed to proceed to Bombay on that day, as had been planned. Accordingly, the three of them were allowed to board the plane.

At Bombay, while the families of Dikshit and Karnik were allowed to go right up to the aircraft at Santa Cruz Airport, the representatives of the press were refused such permission.

As the three survivors alighted from the plane, Captain Dikshit's wife, children and brother and Karnik's fiancee, his parents and brother greeted them. They were then greeted by Mr. B.K.Patel, General Manager and other officials and colleagues of Air India International and by their friends. Twenty-two year old, Miss Kamal, Anant Karnik's fiancee felt that she was the luckiest girl in the world that day. Their marriage was scheduled to take place in Bombay on May 19. Dikshit said he had a broken collar bone and it may take some time before he recovered. All the three survivors wept for joy as soon as they got down from the aircraft. On

Sunday April 17, Mr. A.C.Guzdar, Operation & Engineering Manager of Air India International, issued the following statement at Bombay :

"A report has now been received from the three surviving members of the crew of The *Kashmir Princess* on the events which led to its loss in the China Sea on the 11th April 1955, while on a chartered flight from Hong Kong to Djakarta. The aircraft was flying normally at about 18,000 feet in the pioximity of Natuna Islands when, at about 4.53 pm (local time), a muffled explosion was heard and white smoke began to enter the cabin through the air ducts. The baggage compartment fire warning light came "ON", whereupon, fire extinguishers were immediately discharged into this rapidly to the right wing, while the whole interior of the aircraft, including the pilot's cockpit, filled with thick smoke. Capt D.K.Jatar decided on an immediate landing on water, owing to the damage to the right wing caused by the rapidly spreading fire, the resultant failure of the hydraulic system and the heavy smoke in the cockpit which destroyed visibility. The descent and landing were made under exceptionally difficult conditions. The aircraft touched the water with some force and sank almost immediately."

As I had mentioned earlier in this story, the site of the crash (that is, the Sedanau Island) was obviously the first place visited by the Inquiry Commission on the 15th and 16th April in order to meet the eye-witnesses who had actually seen on April 11, 1955, a burning plane plunging into the sea off Sedanau Island and had spotted the three survivors, brought them to Genting and placed them in the custody of the local authorities at Genting and to record their statements.

After recording the statement of flight Navigator J.C.Pathak at Dum Dum Airport, Calcutta on April 20, 1955, the members of the Inquiry Commission flew from Calcutta to Singapore by B.O.A.C. flight and landed at Singapore at 1230 hours (local time) on April 21.

CONSTELLATION AIRCRAFT

ANNEXURE-9

ANNEXURE - 10

Flight Navigator Sri J. C. Pathak is being examined at Dum Dum Airport by the Indonesian Inquiry Commission. Sri Pathak (extreme right) with his head in sling replying to questions put by the Commission. Mr. Imaswn (Chairman) is on the extreme left.

Pathak Examined In Camera

Enquiry By Indonesian Commission

By A Staff Reporter

One of the three survivors of the ill-fated Air India International Constellation, "Kashmir Princess" Sri J. C. Pathak, Flight Navigator, was examined in camera at Dum Dum airport on Wednesday night by the Indonesian Commission of Inquiry appointed to investigate the crash.

The 5-man Inquiry Commission arrived from Bombay by air after nightfall. The 28-year-old Flight Navigator Sri Pathak with his head plastered arrived at the airport accompanied by his elder brother, a high railway official, a few minutes earlier than the scheduled time of the Commission's arrival. He looked quite fit and exchanged greetings with the members of the Commission and officials of the Air India International.

The members of the Commission who stayed at the airport guest house for the night, were due to leave for Singapore in the early hours of Thursday morning by a B.O.A.C. plane. The Commission is expected to return to Djakarta on April 22.

The Commission comprises: Mr. Imaswan (Chairman), Mr. Hellingers and Dr. M. R. Kummings of the Indonesian Civil Aviation Department, Col. A. K. Mitra, military attache to the Indian Embassy in Indonesia (observer) and Mr. J. Chaves, representing the International Civil Aviation Organisation.

The Consul-General of Indonesia in Calcutta Mr. B. Darusman received the members of the Commission at the airport.

De tuinp van de "Kashmir Princess". De gewonde waarnemer Pathak (rechts) wordt verhoord, door de commissie van onderzoek. V.l.n.r.: R. J. Imaswan, voorzitter, kolonel A. K. Mitra, Indiaas militair attaché te Djakarta en A.J. Chaves van de ICAO.

Chapter 7

FACT-FINDING IN SINGAPORE AND DJAKARTA

The following day the *Singapore Standard*, one of the leading English dailies of Singapore, carried the following news item :

"CRASH INQUIRY TEAM ARRIVES IN SINGAPORE"

"The five man Commission which is carrying out preliminary technical enquiries into the crash of the Air India Constellation on Easter Monday flew into Singapore from Calcutta yesterday 21 April 1955. They visited the scene of the crash last week before they flew to India to question the three survivors".

After arrival in Singapore at 1230 hours on April 21, the Commission had a meeting with the Indian High Commissioner to Malaya at Singapore, Mr. K.M. Raha, Deputy Director General, Civil Aviation, India and Mr. Malhotra, Inspector Accidents, Civil Aviation Directorate, India. Later, they called on the Indonesian Consul General at Singapore.

In its edition of Friday, April 22, the *Singapore Standard* carried the following news item :

"HUSH-HUSH PROBE BY 2 CHINESE OFFICIALS"

"Two Chinese Communist representatives are in Singapore to carry out a hush hush investigation on the Air India Constellation crash with the loss of 16 lives in Indonesian waters on Easter Monday 11 April. They are Mr. Shen Tren and Mr. Gi Khom Tan, both attached to the Communist Chinese Embassy in New Delhi. They arrived at Kelang airport on Tuesday, 19 April 55".

"Red China had alleged that the plane was sabotaged while in Hong Kong".

"On Wednesday morning 20 April 1955, they attended the cremation of one of the crash victims, believed to be one of the minor Bandung-bound Chinese officials".

"Yesterday, they went to the Kelang Airport to wait the arrival of the five-member Commission appointed by the Indonesian Government to investigate the crash".

Early in the morning on Friday April 22, the members of the Inquiry Commission met at Singapore Airport to interrogate the officials concerned with Air Traffic Control (ATC), communication and airport management. To begin with, the Superintendent of the ATC was questioned. The Commission observed that the Superintendent was made aware in advance that The Kashmir Princcess had left Hong Kong airport on the afternoon on April 11 and was scheduled to pass over Singapore Flying Information Region (FIR) and then land at Djakarta airport at about 8 p.m. same day. The Commission requested the Superintendent, to narrate all that he knew about the air crash in the evening of April 11, 1955.

The Superintendent began by clarifying that it was the practice of Singapore ATC to record the time by Greenwich Mean Time (GMT) the time difference being 7½ hours.

The first position report of The *Kashmir Princess* was received by Singapore ATC at 0655 hours GMT (April 11). The next position report was received by the Singapore FIR at 0815 hours GMT and was normal. The subsequent position report (received at 0915 hours GMT) indicated that the aircraft was flying above the clouds at an altitude of 18,000 feet. As far as the Singapore FIR Controller was concerned, the next major communication was received at 0940 hours GMT through high frequency radio telephone which was connected to the Singapore ATC Centre by teleprinter. A teleprinter message was received from Djakarta ATC advising the Singapore FIR Controller that Djakarta ATC had heard MAYDAY signal three times from DEP (that is, The *Kashmir Princess*) at about 0925 hours GMT but no chart of its position was given. In accordance with the prescribed procedures, the Singapore FIR Controller took immediate action by calling upon all their high frequency Wireless Tramission (HF W/T) and Radio Telephone (R/T) operators to establish communication with the aircraft in distress. The RT Station was asked to initiate and transmit distress calls to all the ships sailing in that area. It was also logged that he had asked the Superintendent of Telecommunications at St. Michael to inform all naval stations in the region. The Singapore F.I.R. Controller further consulted with ATCO 1/C of the watch and the RAF Controller and gave all relevant details and last position report of the aircraft. The Singapore ATC requested that the RAF Search and Rescue Organisation be alerted. The time was 0945 hours GMT. The Co-ordination Centre was at Seleter and entirely run by RAF and handled by the Search And Rescue (SAR) Controller at Seleter.

Disaster in the Air : The Crash of the Kashmir Princess 1955 65

At 0954 hours GMT, it was gathered from the RAF Controller that he was able to advise them that rescue had been alerted and that one Sunderland aircraft would be despatched without delay. At the same time, a message was sent to the Centre at Djakarta to confirm the distress call. All other centres were advised of the distress call and were asked to communicate any information which they might pick up. No information came from any centre except from the Djakarta Centre.

Calculations were then made by the RAF Controller based on the last position report of The *Kashmir Princess* at 0915 hours GMT and its MAYDAY distress call at 0925 hours GMT. Information regarding the likely position where the aircraft might have crashed, was passed on to the Rescue Co-ordination Centre (R.C.C.) The Commission observed that there was no proof that the aircraft was within 20 miles or 30 miles of the likely position calculated by the RAF Controller at 0925 hours GMT. (However, it was later proved that the likely position of the crash as calculated by the RAF Controller was within 10 miles of the actual site of the crash). In reply to the Commission's query, the Superintendent, Singapore ATC Centre clarified that the responsibility of the Centre was to ensure that any relevant information passing through the Centre was duly reported to the R.C.C. and to keep the ATC Centres at Djakarta, Hong Kong and Air-India, Bombay, duly informed.

In reply to further queries of the Commission, the Superintendent, Singapore ATC Centre gave the following clarifications :

1. The MAYDAY distress call of The Kashmir Princess was received by the Djakarta ATC who passed on the same to the Singapore ATC Centre at 0940 hours GMT (1655 hours Djakarta time).
2. The MAYDAY distress call of The Kashmir Princess could not be picked up directly by the Singapore ATC Centre. The Radio Telephone (R/T) Station at Singapore was under a different department and not under Singapore ATC Centre. The Singapore R/T Station did not receive the MAYDAY distress call. There was no high frequency (HF) distress frequency, only Very High Frequency (VHF). It was therefore inferred that The Kashmir Princess had followed the normal procedures and had probably transmitted its MAYDAY distress signal on the frequency last used by it.

The Superintendent, further informed the Commission that the first Sunderland aircraft was airborne at 12 hours GMT. The R.C.C. agreed to the request of the authorities of the Indonesian Air Force to detail two aircrafts of the Indonesian Air Force to join the search at 1806 hours

(Djakarta time) on April 11. The Singapore ATC Centre received the following messages on the 12th and 13th April :

Tuesday April 12 : Message received from *m.v. Taype* (belonging to M/s Soon Bee Steamship Co., Singapore) that, on the previous day (April 11), it had observed a plane crashing into the sea at the approximate location 0353 - 108 E and *m.v. Taype* informed the Rescue Co-ordinating Centre at Seleter at 0034 hours GMT.

At 0442 hours GMT, message received from Rescue Co-ordination Centre that the Sunderland aircraft detailed by the RAF had sighted the wreckage of the aircraft as well as a life jacket near the site of the wreckage and that a frigate of the British Navy, *H.M.S.Dampier* was proceeding towards the site of the wreckage.

At 0527 hours GMT, message received via Indonesian Tandjunguban Radio that the aircraft crashed in flames between Djalik Island and Batu Bilis Island and that the local police and local people were searching for survivors.

At 0532 hours GMT message received from m.v. Taype that 3 survivors of the crash had been brought to Genting.

At 0700 hours, message received from m.v. Taype that the survivors of the air crash were the First Officer, Navigator and Ground Engineer with slight injuries.

At 0934 hours GMT, measage received from the Rescue Co-ordination Centre that arrangements had been made for the three survivors to be transferred from *m.v. Taype* to *H.M.S.Dampier* to receive medical aid.

At 1057 hours GMT, message received from *m. v. Taype* that the three survivors had been transferred at sea to the *Dampier.*

Wednesday April 13 : At 0221 hours GMT, message received from the R.C.C. that one RAF Sunderland aircraft and one Indonesian Air Force Dakota were continuing to search for other survivors along with the *Dampier.*

At 0930 hours GMT, message received from the R.C.C. that *H.M.S. Dampier* was carrying out diving operations at the site of the crash.

The next person to be interrogated by the Commission at the Singapore Airport on April 22 was Commander C.R.K.Roe, Commander of the Royal Naval frigate, *H.M.S.Dampier* based at Singapore Naval Base. The gist of the statement made by Commander C.R.K.Roe was as follows:

On receipt of an important and urgent message at 10-08 p.m. (Singapore time) on April 11, from the Flag Officer, Malaya, he sailed from Singapore Naval Base at 11-30 p.m. (Singapore time) and proceeded to Natuna Islands, reaching there the following day (that is, Tuesday, April 12) at 0530 hours (Singapore time).

Disaster in the Air : The Crash of the Kashmir Princess 1955

On the way, he maintained radio contact with the RAF search aircraft as well as with *m. v. Taype*. He received a signal from the latter that she had taken on board three survivors of the air crash. He arranged to meet *m.v. Taype* westward of Sedanau Island, just outside the Indonesian territorial waters approximately 4 miles off Sedanau Island. At that point (that is, in Malayan waters), the three survivors were transferred from *m. v. Taype* to *H.M.S. Dampier*. By the time they were taken on board, it had already become quite dark and hence there was no point in going towards the site of the crash, as it would not have been possible to carry out any meaningful search operation in darkness.

At about 0600 hours on the following day (that is, April 13) *H.M.S. Dampier* proceeded to the site of the crash and started searching the area. Three boats of the ship were deployed for the search operations at the site as well as at nearby areas and islands. These boats carried out searches on all the beaches of the islands near the site of the crash and also met fishermen and local villagers of those islands to ascertain whether they had seen any other survivors of the crash. Another boat went to Genting to pick up the District Officer and then to proceed to the site of the crash to see the wreckage. The boat reached the site at 1100 hours. On April 13, Commander Roe offered the services of his divers and the offer was promptly and gratefully accepted by the District Officer of Genting. The boat came alongside the ship and collected the divers, who started search operations at 12-30 p.m. and continued till dark. During the diving operations, three bodies came to the surface. It was not possible to establish whether the bodies were in the aircraft or had been caught in the wreckage. While the identity of two of the three bodies could be established on the basis of the papers found on them, the identity of the third body could not be established, since there was nothing on that body except the tattered remains of a pair of trousers. The three bodies were taken on board the ship. Two pieces of wreckage, presumably from the galley portion of the aircraft, were collected by one of the fishermen who handed them over to the ship's divers in their boat.

The District Officer came aboard the ship at about 5 p.m. and enquired whether there was anything further to be done, as he was planning to return to Genting in the evening. On being informed that there was nothing more to be done, he appeared to be satisfied.

Regarding the three survivors on board the ship, the crash being still fresh in their memory, they were in a state of shock thinking about the traumatic experience they had to go through. Their injuries were such that they could be attended to on the ship. Otherwise, there was nothing serious in their condition and therefore it was not considered necessary to transfer them from *H.M.S. Dampier* to the RAF Sunderland aircraft which was a seaplane.

The things salvaged from the wreckage of The *Kashmir Princess* as well as the papers found on the three bodies were handed over to the Indonesian Naval Police for safe custody.

H.M.S. Dampier was at the site of the crash almost 48 hours after the crash. It was felt that if there had been any other survivors, they would have been spotted by fishermen and villagers of the nearby islands. Enquiries made by the ship's divers from the fishermen and villagers revealed that they had not spotted any other survivor. Therefore, there was no point in the *Dampier* prolonging its stay at the site of the crash and the ship left at about 7 p.m. At that time, two boats of the Indonesian Navy were at the site of the crash and their divers were continuing the search of the area.

Immediately after completing the interrogation of Commander C.R.K.Roe, the Inquiry Commission interrogated Mr. W.D.Hughes of the Royal Navy and acting Commissioned Boatswain of the *Dampier*, whose deposition before the Commission was as follows :

At about 11.30 a.m. (Singapore time) on Tuesday, April 12, the Captain of The *Dampier* sent for him and instructed him to get the diving equipment ready. The *Dampier* then proceeded to the site of the wreckage of The *Kashmir Princess* where two Indonesian naval ships had already been secured to the wreckage of the aircraft by their own divers.

After diving to a depth of 30 feet, Hughes observed that the round nose of the aircraft was missing. He then proceeded along the starboard wing of the aircraft for about 15 feet. On closer examination of the starboard wing, it appeared that it had broken off, still attached to the fuselage, but pushed well forward. Since visibility at that depth was about 5-6 feet only, he could not see the engines. He considered it dangerous to go aft of the starboard wing and therefore returned to the nose of the aircraft. He noticed that the two windows on the starboard side of the cockpit with their windscreen wipers were intact. The concave bulk-head aft was damaged. While floating round to the port-side of the cockpit, he could read the letters "KASHMIR". The port-wing appeared to have been thrown forward by the impact of the starboard wing with the water. He did not venture out to the port-wing since his primary task was to locate and to recover the bodies of the victims trapped in the wreckage of the aircraft, and not to make an assessment of damage.

Hughes felt that the best approach for entry into the aircraft was from the top of the fuselage. He had not searched the whole of the cockpit. He also did not find any of the emergency doors on the fuselage open.

Disaster in the Air : The Crash of the Kashmir Princess 1955

Hughes then surfaced and another diver descended into the water. Visibility was worsening but telephone communications between the divers and the crew on the surface was good and there appeared to be no cause for worry. Hughes narrated to the Commission what the diver had reported to him after returning to the surface.

The second diver landed on top of the aircraft and through a hole, entered into what appeared to be the Navigator's Compartment. He floated forward into the cockpit and reported that he could not find any body in the cockpit. He then worked his way aft and noticed some instruments which he presumed to be in the Navigator's Compartment. At that time, three bodies surfaced in the vicinity of the rescue ships. The bodies had inflated lifejackets on them. It was presumed that the bodies were disturbed inside the wreckage and then got dislodged by the buoyancy caused by the hose of the diver. The diver then reported that he had found a dinghy with a radio transmitter attached, with the words "Signal Corps" stencilled on the yellow material. On instruction from the surface, he continued to move aft and reported that he had seen a large hole in the main deck of the aircraft which was made of thick plywood. He crossed the hole and felt that the flooring seemed to go up almost vertically. He later found out that it was not the floor that went up but the bulkhead that was slightly tilted aft. The diver surmised that the large hole was presumably the position of the main fracture on the fuselage, on the basis of an observation earlier made by the Ground Engineer Karnik that the fuselage had fractured at the top. Diving operations undertaken to locate and examine the wreckage of sunken ships and aircraft are generally regarded as hazardous operations. In this case, yet another inhibiting factor was the extremely poor visibility. It was, therefore, felt that asking the diver to move further aft inside the aircraft would be risky. The diver was called to come up to the surface to carry out an external examination of the fuselage portion of the wreckage.

The Captain of The *Dampier* received instructions at about 1730 hours from the Naval Base at Singapore (that is, about half an hour before darkness set in) to return to base. The second diver, who had dived to the bottom, was instructed to come to the surface and then to return to the ship.

Hughes had reported that, in his opinion, the fuselage was in one piece, but was badly fractured. The hole observed in the deck was smaller than the hole observed on the top of the aircraft. One of the Indonesian ships had a line secured to a double wheel not far from the port side of the cockpit. The wheel itself was positioned in such a way that Hughes did not like to say that it came from the port wing.

The Inquiry Commission then interrogated Captain E.Hebblewhite, master of the *Taype* belonging to Soon Bee Steamship Company, Singapore, on April 22. The deposition of Captain Hebblewhite was as follows:

The *Taype* received the SOS message from Djakarta at 8 p.m. on Monday April 11, indicating the position of the air crash. Since the position given was more or less in the same direction as the *Taype* was proceeding she merely carried on and eventually called at Genting. The last position given by The *Kashmir Princess* (i.e. about ten minutes before she gave the MAYDAY signal) was 04.30° North, 108.20° East. The *Taype* arrived at Genting at 0635 hours on April 12. After making enquiries, the captain gathered from the local inhabitants that they had seen a burning aircraft, covered in smoke, crashing into the sea. That gave an indication of the site of the crash. The captain marked the position on his chart and sent a report to Singapore ATC. The inhabitants also reported having picked up some items of luggage - books, papers and a few life jackets. They had not seen any survivors. They would be going out that very morning (that is, April 12) for a further search. Pursuant to the message sent by Capt Hebblewhite to the Singapore ATC at 0900 hours on April 12, three RAF Sunderland aircraft were hovering over the site of the crash and making a thorough search for two or three hours and thereafter flew at a very low altitude around the smaller islands in the vicinity. The distress call had also been repeated by the Rescue Co-ordination Centre at Seleter, giving the last position as reported by the Kashmir Princess before it crashed into the sea.

The first message about the MAYDAY distress call of The *Kashmir Princess* was received from the Indonesian authorities at Djakarta at 2000 hours on April 11, (that is, about three hours after the approximate time of the crash). The *Taype* did not receive the MAYDAY call directly from The *Kashmir Princess* , presumably because of the difference in wave-lengths. The Indonesian authorities at Djakarta had communicated the message to all ships sailing in that area, giving them the date, time and approximate position of the crash and requesting them to be on the look out and to convey any information which they might gather.

Having gathered that the ship Marudu was coming from North Borneo to assist in the search, Capt Hebblewhite sent a message to the captain of the Marudu not to proceed to the original position of the crash, conveyed by the Indonesian authorities at Djakarta because that was wrong information. The message gave the approximate location of the crash with the details of the items that had been picked up the previous day; and also contained a warning to the captain of the Marudu that the area proposed to be searched by her was inside shoal patches.

By April 12, several small boats were searching the area surrounding the site of the crash. The *Taype* had anchored at Genting as it was not possible for big ships to go into that area since it was inside shoal patches.

At 1245 hours on April 12, Capt Hebblewhite gathered that a local *praw* had brought three Indian survivors with serious injuries (it was reported that one of the survivors had a broken neck) to the jetty at Genting, Capt Hebblewhite sent the following message to the Singapore Air Traffic Control (ATC) :

"Air Control Singapore inform Sunderland RAF HDNZ 5813 survivors at Genting can you land near ship *Taype* they require medical attention urgently reply - Master *Taype*".

The Captain then instructed his chief officer to go ashore to interview the three survivors at the jetty and report on their condition. The Captain also sent a member of his crew to buy clothing for the three survivors as they were reported to be lying on the jetty in their underwear.

In the meantime, The *Taype* received a message from Base Operations, R.C.C., Seleter (Singapore), that The *Dampier*, was speeding to the assistance of The *Taype* and was expected to be alongside her by 1000 hours G.M.T.

The Chief Officer returned to the ship. At the request of Dikshit, the Chief Officer sent a message to the office of Air India International at Bombay to the effect that Dikshit had a broken collar bone and the navigator (J.C.Pathak) had a split scalp and severe leg abrasions. The Chief Officer also sent a message to Singapore ATC reporting that three survivors (i.e. First Officer Dikshit, the Navigator and the Ground Engineer) had been contacted at the jetty of Genting.

Dikshit appeared to be certain that there were three more survivors floating on the sea somewhere and this was also conveyed in the message sent by The *Taype* to the office of Air India International, Bombay.

At 1450 hours (April 12, 1955), The *Taype* received a message from The *Dampier* to the effect that she would arrive at Salor Island (which was located at a distance of about 7-8 miles from the site of the crash) with medical assistance and that she was in touch with the RAF Sunderland rescue aircraft. The *Dampier* gave her position, so that The *Taype* could intercept her. Capt Hebblewhite again deputed his Chief Officer to go ashore in order to arrange to speed up the formalities for clearance of the three survivors and to bring them on board. At 1445 hours (April 12, 1955), the Captain sent the following message to the Singapore A.T.C.:

"Survivors were still ashore and would meet him south of Sedanau Island near the channel entrance". In the same message, the Captain also mentioned that one survivor had a broken collar bone and another survivor had a split scalp and severe leg abrasions.

At 1515 hours, the Captain of The *Taype* despatched a message on behalf of the Wedana of Genting addressed to the Bhupati Tanjong Priang and Wedana Tarempa to the effect that she would be taking the three survivors on board and would be meeting the ship *Darmpier*, which had been sent from Singapore with all medical facilities.

At 1600 hours, the three survivors were taken on board The *Taype* and after obtaining clearance of the port authorities at Genting, she left the port. The Captain sent a message to the *Dampier* to the effect that she was leaving Genting via South Channel and would meet the *Dampier* at sea.

On account of the fairly large volume of wireless communications from several other ships sailing in that area. The *Taype* received two messages late and that too after a lot of difficulty. One message was from the *Dampier* suggesting that the three survivors should not be moved from Genting having regard to the serious nature of the injuries sustained by two of them. This message was received when the three survivors were already on board. The second message, received late, was from the R.A.F. Sunderland rescue aircraft stating that they were unable to establish contact with The *Taype* since they could not get on the wave-length of the ship's wireless system.

The *Taype* sighted the *Dampier* at 1645 hours and made radio contact with her at 1719 hours. Both the ships stopped in mid-sea and came side by side when the three survivors were transferred from The *Taype* to The *Dampier*.

The Captain of The *Dampier* sent a message to the Singapore ATC stating that The *Taype* had transferred the three survivors to his ship and that she would commence search at the site of the crash at daylight the following day.

On Saturday April 23, the Inquiry Commission interrogated Squadron Leader A.Craig; Royal Air Force, Incharge of the Rescue Co-ordination Centre (R.C.C.), Singapore at Singapore Airport, Kelang. The deposition of Sq. Ldr. Craig was as follows :

Sq. Ldr. Craig was responsible for the R.C.C. at Seleter. He was called to the R.C.C. shortly after 1720 hrs on April 11, with the message that a Lockheed Constellation aircraft had transmitted a MAYDAY message from somewhere to the east of Singapore. He went to the R.C.C. immediately and learnt that the Lockheed Constellation aircraft was an Air India airliner on a flight from Hong Kong to Djakarta. The aircraft had transmitted a routine position report at 0916 hours GMT and about nine minutes later it had transmitted its MAYDAY message thrice and thereafter there had been no communication from the aircraft. Sq. Ldr. Craig immediately alerted the Search and Rescue (S.A.R) stand-by aircraft and the high speed launch which they had at Seleter. He spoke to Singapore Airport, Kelang, and got all the information gathered by him upto that time, verified once again. Since there was no communication from the aircraft after its MAYDAY message, contingency plans had to be made. The stand-by aircraft and the high-speed launch were ordered to move towards a datum which the R.C.C. at Seleter had constructed. The launch was sent at about 1825 hours to a holding position which was merely a convenient spot between Seleter and a spot in the sea where the aircraft was most likely to have ditched, in the vicinity of the China Rock. The stand-by Sunderland aircraft took off at about 1845 hours and proceeded towards a datum position based on the last transmission (that is, prior to the MAYDAY message) made by the aircraft. The datum position had been plotted ahead of the last reported position for nine minutes which was the duration of time between the aircraft's routine transmission and its MAYDAY message. It was known that the Sunderland aircraft would be there until dark and would be carrying out a "square" search, using five miles visibility distance. The briefing to the Sunderland was to maintain a watch on HFDF frequency as alloted during the day and a different frequency for the night. She was further ordered to fire a "green verey light" cartridge every five minutes and also at turning points. The idea was that if the survivors were in a dinghy they would have their own cartridges and on sighting the verey lights of the Sunderland aircraft, the survivors would fire one in return and thereby reveal their position. Later in the evening, Sq. Ldr. Craig despatched the high speed launch from its holding position at China Rock to Pulau Medai.

At that stage of his deposition, Sq. Ldr. Craig produced a map of the area of the crash and explained the rescue operations carried out. Craig had also sent messages to all shipping at 2000 hours April 11, containing information of the crash.

The R.C.C. got in touch with the Naval Dockyard in Singapore, urging it to deploy *H.M.S. Dampier* as quickly as possible. She sailed at 2300 hours (Singapore time) on April 11, towards the area of the crash. Early in the morning on April 12, two RAF Sunderland aircraft were detailed to carry out the search of that area using one mile visibility.

On the assumption that the aircraft would have tried to ditch at a point closest to land (that is, the shores of the islands in that area) the R.C.C. at Seleter detailed two Lincolns on the track to Serawak which was presumed to be the location where the aircraft might have ditched. The R.C.C. received information through Singapore Airport, Kelang that a PBY and C-47 Indonesian Airforce aircraft would like to participate in the search. The R.C.C. advised them to cover the Serawak and surrounding areas. The idea was to cover as large an area as was possible for carrying out the search operations.

On receipt of a message from The *Taype*, reporting sightings by locals, R.C.C., diverted the second Sunderland aircraft to make a visual search around Natuna Island and Genting. At that point of time, the R.C.C. received a message from the high-speed launch that it would be reaching the site of the crash within about an hour. The R.C.C. advised the high speed launch to return to Singapore, since the *Dampier* was already on the way to the site of the crash. The R.C.C. requested the *Dumpier* to communicate with their high speed launch and to advise it to return to Singapore. The R.C.C. also ordered all the Sunderland aircraft to close position and to report on the possibility of one of the aircrafts alighting at Genting to verify the reports of the inhabitants of Natuna Islands about picking up some items of luggage from near the site of the crash.

The R.C.C. received a further message from The *Taype* at 0930 hours that, as per eye witness reports, the burning aircraft had crashed into the sea at a point between Djalik Island and Batu Bilis Island, four miles off Sedenau Island. Yet another message at 1010 hours advised that the wreckage of the aircraft had been located (with map reference) at a depth of about 6 to 8 fathoms in sea water. This was later confirmed by the Sunderland aircraft. Till that time, there was no report from any quarter that any survivor was located, but that the police and local people were continuing the search.

After having come to know that the wreckage of the aircraft had been located and that the *Dampier* was proceeding towards the site of the crash, R.C.C., Seleter, deployed yet another Sunderland aircraft at 1251 hours (April 12) to establish a link between the site of the wreckage and the *Dampier*. At 1300 hours the Sunderland sighted one white box and a couple of small objects (yellow in colour) in the vicinity of the site of the crash. At 1317 hours The *Taype* sent the following message to the RAF Sunderland aircraft (air radio) :

"Three survivors at Genting. Can you land near ship ? They require medical attention urgently".

At 1400 hours the two Sunderland aircraft, which had been recalled, were debriefed. The site of the crash had been indicated to them by a small launch circling the site of the crash and a person in a canoe had held up a life jacket (yellow in colour) and a travelling trunk. At 0957 hours (April 13, 1955) *H.M.S. Dampier* sent the following message (prepared by Dikshit) to the R.C.C. requesting them to pass on the same to the office of

Air India International at Kelang, Singapore :

"Aircraft crashed with port wing on fire and hydraulics failure, broke into three parts on hitting water. Cabin section sank immediately. Of the three survivors, two escaped from the cockpit and the third escaped from the aft part".

At 1310 hours (April 13, 1955), the Royal Navy Base at Singapore sent the following message to the Captain of the *Dampier.*

"If on completion of daylight search today Wednesday 13th you do not consider further search of any use, you should return to Singapore exceeding economical speed as requisite. The Indian High Commission at Singapore has been given full information."

The Inquiry Commission observed that The *Taype* had asked the Sunderland whether it could alight and pick up the survivors, to which there appeared to be no response from the Sunderland. Sq. Ldr. Craig clarified that according to the regulations in force, it was only on the specific authority of the R.C.C. and only in the absence of any other surface craft nearby that the Sunderland aircraft would have been permitted to alight. Further, on being asked as to whether the alighting of the Sunderland aircraft would have resulted in the saving of life, the Captain of The *Dampier* had replied that he had a doctor on board capable of rendering requisite medical assistance to the three survivors. Hence, the Sunderland aircraft did not alight.

After the deposition of Sq. Ldr. Craig on Saturday, April 23, 1955, the Inquiry Commission interrogated Flight Lieutenant (FLT.LT.) A.W.G.Thomas, Royal Air Force, Seleter, Singapore, whose deposition was as follows :

At the start of the proceedings, Mr. Imawan, Chairman of the Inquiry Commission, observed that Sq. Ldr. Craig had made a detailed statement. However, the Commission would still like to know what action was taken on the message sent by The *Taype* to the Sunderland aircraft requesting her to alight on the water to pick up the three survivors who were on board *m.v. Taype.*

FLT. LT. Thomas replied that The *Taype's* message was not received by the Sunderland. The aircraft was the first to take off after the receipt of the distress call by the R.C.C., Seleter. She took off at 1845 hours and proceeded straight towards the datum initially given as the position of the distress call, somewhere close to Natuna Island, with instructions to do expanding square search on the night type pattern at 5,000 feet or as near to it as could be managed. The Sunderland aircraft did not receive any message from The *Taype* during the night search.

Their Sunderland aircraft was relieved at 0230 hours (April 12,

1955) by a substitute Sunderland aircraft. During the square search carried out at night, the aircraft fired green verey lights but did not see or hear anything. The visibility in that area was excellent at that time. The search was carried out as per regulations laid down, that is from 5,000 feet or as close to that as was possible, to give maximum visibility, firing verey lights at the interval of five minutes to enable possible survivors to spot the aircraft and to respond by firing their own verey lights.

The Singapore A.T.C./the R.C.C. Seleter had sent a message to the Sunderland aircraft that, as per information gathered by them The *Kashmir Princess* was carrying two red vereys, two green and two blue vereys plus one dinghy. The crew of the Sunderland carried out a radar search at the same time, assuming that the survivors were perhaps equipped with radar. However, the crew of the Sunderland did not pick up any sign of anything at all.

FLT. LT. Thomas stated that his aircraft was associated with the search on the following day also, that is, Wednesday April 13, 1955. By that time, The *Dampier* was in position and the exact location of the wreckage of The *Kashmir Princess* had also been found out. The crew of the Sunderland set course at first light on April 13 and proceeded straight towards the site of the crash and carried out a low-level search to locate survivors, on the open sea as well as on the beaches of all the islands in the vicinity of the site of the crash but did not see anything at all other than a ship near the location of the wreckage of the aircraft. The crew could clearly see into the water, the surrounding area, the coral reef etc. and the crew also saw from their chart that the depth of the water at the location of the wreckage of the crash was about five fathoms, that is, about thirty feet. The crew also saw the tell-tale signs of oil floating on the surface of the water near the location of the wreckage.

The deposition of FLT. LT. Thomas marked the completion of the interrogation by the Inquiry Commission of all the persons who could throw some light on the crash of The *Kashmir Princess*.

After having heard all the evidences at Genting and Singapore, it became clear to the Inquiry Commission that the explosion in The *Kashmir Princess* was followed by all kinds of emergencies which the captain and the crew of The *Kashmir Princess* could possibly have faced, namely, a serious fire that threatened to burn off the right wing (starboard wing) at any moment, failure of the hydraulic system, failure of the electrical system, failure of the wireless communication system, partial loss of control in the cockpit, dense smoke in the cockpit which reduced visibility to almost nil during the most critical stage of descent. Despite all the efforts of the Captain and the Co-Pilot to level off the aircraft for ditching, it hurtled down in a right hand turn and hit the water. The flaps could not be brought into use on account of the failure of the hydraulic system. It was inferred that the aircraft took at least 5 to 6 minutes to descend from an altitude of 18,000 feet, while under partial loss of control, the tip of the starboard wing hit the water and broke up on impact.

Earlier, on Monday April 18, the Prime Minister of India, Mr. Nehru, had sent the following note to the Indian Ambassador in Djakarta :

"I have seen several telegrams from Singapore and New Delhi regarding salvage operations of the Air India Constellation. Inquiry is made in this as to what the Indonesian Government is doing. What is the position ? This is a very urgent matter, as delay will nullify any efforts made. I presume you are in touch with the Indonesian Government."

sd/-
(J.Nehru)
18.04.55
Camp : Bandung

Shri B.F.H.B. Tyabji
Colonel A.K.Mitra

Prime Minister Nehru had also received several cables and telegrams from Mrs. Jatar and also from the relatives of other missing crew members to use his good offices to expedite the tracing of their whereabouts. It appeared that Mrs. Jatar strongly believed that her husband was still alive and was perhaps lost somewhere in the Great Natuna Islands.

With the mounting pressure from Prime Minister Nehru, Government of India and Air India International, the Inquiry Commission decided that immediate measures should be taken to salvage the wreckage of the aircraft in order to recover any bodies which may be found trapped in the wreckage. It was a matter of concern that the body of the Commander Capt Jatar had not yet been found.

The Government of India had, through India's High Commissioner at Singapore, Mr. R.K.Tandon, approached the Royal Navy at Singapore for help and assistance in the salvage operations for recovering the wreckage of The *Kashmir Princess* from the site of the crash.

When the Inquiry Commission was in session at the Singapore Airport, India's High Commissioner at Singapore Mr. R.K.Tandon, arrived at Singapore Airport and informed the Commission that he had received special authorisation of the Govt. of India to approach the Royal Navy at

Singapore to seek their assistance in the salvage operations. He enquired from the Chairman of the Commission as to whether there was any objection from the Indonesian authorities to the proposal to associate the Royal Navy in the salvage operations.

After quick internal consultations, the Chairman of the Commission informed Mr. Tandon that while there was no objection to associate the Royal Navy in the salvage operations, the ships of the Royal Navy should carry out the salvage operations under the supervision of the Indonesian Navy. The Chairman of the Commission also informed Mr. Tandon that the vessels of the Indonesian Navy including salvage vessel The *Telantik* had already sailed and were expected to be at the site of the crash very soon.

The authorities of the Royal Navy at Singapore placed their salvage vessel *H.M.S. Barford* at the disposal of the Inquiry Commission with immediate effect. The *Barford* was ready to sail immediately.

After a brief meeting of the Commission with Mr. Tandon, officials of the Directorate General of Civil Aviation, India and General Manager of Air India International at Singapore, it was decided that Mr. Malhotra, Accident Inspector, Civil Aviation of India and Mr. Appuswamy, Chief Engineering Inspector, Air India, should proceed to the site of the crash in The *Barford* along with the Indonesian Naval Attache at Singapore. The *Barford* sailed for Natuna Island at 1400 hours on April 24, 1955.

The Inquiry Commission completed the interrogation of witnesses at the Singapore Airport by 1600 hours on April 23, 1955. The members of the Commission left Singapore for Djakarta by Qantas Airways flight at 0800 hours on Sunday April 24 and arrived at Djakarta at 1000 hours. Mr. K.M. Raha, Deputy Director General, Civil Aviation, Govt. of India, New Delhi, also travelled by the same flight.

On Monday April 25, the Commission had a series of meetings starting with Dr. Sugato, Director General, Civil Aviation, Indonesia at 0700 hours, followed by the meeting with Dr. M.S.Kamminga, Operation Manager, Garuda Indonesian Airways at 1100 hours which continued till late in the evening. In the course of these meetings, it was decided that the members of the Commission should leave Djakarta on Thursday, April 28, allowing a couple of days for the salvage vessels of the Royal Navy and the Indonesian Navy to get into position at the site of the crash. Accordingly, we made arrangements to fly from Djakarta to Tandjung Penang and from there to proceed to the site of the crash by a vessel of the Indonesian Navy.

We decided to complete the interrogations on Monday April 25, (including the personnel in the Djakarta F.I.R.). The deposition of Mr. Didi Widjajabradja, Radio Operator, Radio Station, Civil Aviation, Kamajoran, Djakarta was as follows :

On April 11, he was on duty from 1300 hours to 1830 hours, as a long-range radio-telephone (R/T) operator, alongwith three colleagues. At 0815 hours GMT he heard, very faintly, VTDEP (that is, the aircraft the *Kashmir Princess*) being transferred from Saigon F.I.R. to Singapore F.I.R. The position report passed by the aircraft was also heard by him very faintly. Then he heard the aircraft requesting Singapore F.I.R. to pass the message to Djakarta F.I.R. regarding night landing facilities which was done. He then called the aircraft through long range R/T and asked whether the aircraft had received the message from Singapore F.I.R. The aircraft replied in the affirmative.

Next, he received a request from the Airport Manager, Djakarta to enquire whether Mr. Chou en-Lai, Prime Minister of the People's Republic of China, was on board the aircraft. The reply from the aircraft was in the negative. Even though the exchange of communications had ended, he did not close down the R/T.

At about 0925 hours GMT (about 1655 hours Djakarta time) he heard MAYDAY, this is DEP, once only. He called Djakarta A.T.C. to the radio set. Then MAYDAY was heard once again, the "strength" of the speaker was 2-3 on R/T. After the ATC officer (Mr. Suparto) came, they both heard "all stations repeat all stations MAYDAY DEP" They both waited for a short while to see whether the position of the aircraft would be transmitted, but there was no further transmission.

He called the aircraft : "VT-DEP, this is Djakarta, do you hear me"? He repeated the call thrice but there was no reply from the aircraft. Since he had some doubt, he called Singapore A.T.C. "Singapore, this is Djakarta, do you hear me ?" Singapore A.T.C. replied : "Go ahead". Then he asked : "Have you heard MAYDAY three times about 0925 Z ?" Singapore ATC replied in the negative. Then he asked the Singapore ATC for the last position of the aircraft VT-DEP. The reply was "04°-30° N 108° 20'E at 0915 Z" . Thereafter, he heard Singapore A.T.C. calling Saigon A.T.C. and another station, possibly Kuching, enquiring whether they had heard MAYDAY from the aircraft. He heard Saigon A.T.C. replying in the negative and he could also hear radio communication between Singapore A.T.C. and an aircraft in fight. He kept a watch on all the four frequencies and passed on information about all that had transpired till then, to Djakarta A.T.C.

In reply to the Commission's query, Mr. Didi clarified that he had called the officer of the Djakarta A.T.C., Mr. Suparto to the radio set to listen to the transmission just to make sure that what he had heard was correct.

Thereafter, the Commission interviewed the following personnel : Mr. Julius Baker, ATC Controller, Civil Aviation, Kamajoran; and Mr. R.Pelsmaker, Despatcher, ATC Centre, Kamajoran. They did not have anything new or important to say. However, Mr. Baker stated that he had alerted through A.U.R.I. (Indonesian Airforce Headquarters), the Search and Rescue Centre, Kamajoran regarding the MAYDAY heard from the aircraft.

The Commission collected the following report on Search and Rescue (SAR) action of the Indonesian Airforce for The *Kashmir Princess* including the record on search and rescue operations initiated in Djakarta (F.I.R.) :

Introductory : The *Kashmir Princess* met with an accident on a flight Hong Kong - Djakarta, when carrying a party of China Peoples Republic Delegation.

Communication/Information : At 04110915 Z the aircraft reported position at 0430 N 10820 E and 10 minutes later (041 1925Z) transmitted MAYDAY called three times after which there was no more communication with VT-DEP.

Receipt of Information : Information concerning the accident mentioned above was passed by the Secretary-General, Ministry of Foreign Affairs, Government of Indonesia to the Chief of Staff, Indonesian Airforce (AURI) at 1630 hours (local time).

Collection of data : Immediately all data were collected concerning the location where the aircraft was expected to have crashed.

Preparation of rescue team : The same evening a rescue team of the Indonesian Airforce was set up.

Flights : Since it was late in the evening already and the aerodromes in the neighbourhood of the crash position of the aircraft were not equipped with night-landing facilities, departure of the AURI aircrafts had to be deferred till early next morning (12 April).

On 12 April, Lieut. O.Dani, took off at about 03.19 hours (local time) for Natuna Island via Singkwang, where he landed at 07.30 hours.

Disaster in the Air : The Crash of the Kashmir Princess 1955

After refuelling, the plane again took off (after about 3 ½ hours) to the location where VT-DEP had given its last position, viz Salor Island. When the aircraft approached Natuna Island, it received instructions to fly to Sedanau Island area. It circled over that area for 45 minutes along with a RAF Sunderland aircraft, but nothing was found. The aircraft then flew to its former destination and about an hour later, it received instructions to fly to Sedanau Island again, where it met PBY aircraft. Every spot where smoke was seen and all areas where it was suspected that the aircraft could have crashed were searched but nothing was found. At 04.30 hours (local time), the aircraft returned to Singkwang. The same day, at 0815 hours, a flying boat under Lieut. Nurprapto took off from Halim Air Base for Natuna. The aircraft reached the island at 1330 hours. Extensive search was carried out in the areas of Sedanau, Salor and Great Natuna Islands but nothing could be seen. In the meantime the aircraft received the position where The Kashmir Princess may have crashed, as 0353 N 10758 E. The aircraft flew over that area for about 1 1/2 hours. East of reference given, the water was found to be of dark-brown colour. The flying boat landed at that place at 1415 hours and got indications from local fishermen that VT-DEP had actually crashed there. As the waves were high and the wind was strong, the flying boat could not anchor and therefore took off again. At 1430 hours, the aircraft landed at its destination, Pontianak.

On 13 April, at 0730 hours, an Indonesian Airforce Dakota took off for Sedanau, where it met PBY, which intended to land at Genting. In that area, there was a RAF Sunderland aircraft, one Indonesian Naval (ALRI) vessel and several other Indonesian vessels. The aircraft circled over the islands to search for survivors on the shores but nothing was found. Communication was established with the PBY which had landed already and at that time instructions were received from base to return to Halim Air Base.

At 0730 hours, another Indonesian aircraft took off for Natuna and landed at Genting at 1000 hours. Capt (Dr.) Salamun and Lt. Gan Sing Liep went ashore, where they collected documents and material recovered from VT-DEP by fishermen and local police. They also received information that the inhabitants had seen the aircraft at 04111700 (local time) on fire and plunging into the sea. On 12 April, early in the morning, three Indians had received first-aid from fishermen and were brought to Genting, where they received medical assistance from The *Taype*. The PBY, a British vessel which was anchored and tried to establish communication by means of light signals but could not establish radio communication. The PBY on return journey to Pontianak, received information that The *Taype* wanted immediate medical assistance for the survivors.

14 April 55 : The Accident Investigation Committee landed at Pontianak Airforce Base at 1430 hours. Due to the late hour, it was decided to fly the Commission next morning to Genting.

15 April 55 : At 0830 hours, the Commission took off by flying boat *Catalina* (AURI) and landed at Genting at 1100 hours. The Commission stayed at Genting for the night. The *Catalina* returned to the base as anchoring at Genting was not possible due to strong wind blowing and there was no buoy available.

16 April 1955 : 0915 hours, The *Catalina* landed at Genting. The Commission left Genting in the afternoon and landed at Kamajoran Airfield at 1700 hours.

With the collection of the above report, the Inquiry Commission had completed its work in Djakarta and was in readiness to move on to the next phase of its investigations.

On the successful conclusion of the Afro-Asian Conference at Bandung, the Indian Premier, Jawaharlal Nehru returned to Djakarta (Tuesday, April 26). The Prime Minister drove straight to the Indian Chancery and after meeting all the officers and staff of the Indian Embassy, he went round the Chancery building. Thereafter, he met Ambassador Tyabji and myself in the Ambassador's office. Mr. S.Dutt, I.C.S. the Secretary-General at Delhi's Ministry of External Affairs, New Delhi, was also present.

The Prime Minister apprised us of what the Chinese Premier Mr. Chou en-Lai had told him in confidence at Bandung regarding the crash of the Indian aircraft carrying the advance party of the Chinese Delegation to Djakarta on April 11, 1955. Mr. Chou en-Lai had mentioned that even before the Chinese Delegation left Peking for Hong Kong, the Government of the People's Republic of China had learned through intelligence reports, that there was a plot to create mischief and to cause harm to the members of the Chinese Delegation on their arrival at Hong Kong Airport to board the Air India plane (which had been chartered by the Chinese Government). The Chinese Government had promptly brought this to the notice of the British Embassy at Peking requesting them to alert the British authorities at Hong Kong and to provide protection to the members of the Chinese Delegation. Mr. Chou en-Lai had further mentioned that some countries disliked the idea of Communist China discussing on an equal footing the problems of mutual concern with the leaders of other democratic Afro-Asian countries. Therefore, they had hatched a plot, with the connivance of secret agents

Disaster in the Air : The Crash of the Kashmir Princess 1955

of U.S.A. and Formosa to sabotage the Air India aircraft and thus thwart the Afro-Asian Conference at Bandung. Mr. Chou en-Lai was certain that Americans and the Government of Formosa had deliberately engineered the sabotage of the Air India aircraft. Mr. Chou en-Lai had urged that utmost care must be taken while salvaging the wreckage of the aircraft from the sea so that the mystery of the air crash could be solved. The Prime Minister then asked me about the work done by the Inquiry Commission till that time and about the action plan for salvaging the wreckage of the aircraft from the sea.

I gave him a resumé of the visit of the Inquiry Commission to Port Genting where the statements of three eye-witnesses had been recorded, then the flights to Bombay and Calcutta, where the statements of the three survivors of the crash had been recorded; and to Singapore and Djakarta where the statements of other relevant persons had been recorded. The Prime Minister was happy to know that the members of the Commission had called on Mrs. Jatar at Bombay to express their sympathies and condolences to her. According to reports from the Natuna Islands, the wreckage of the aircraft was found strewn over an area of a quarter of a square mile in the sea and hence it was taking time to salvage the different parts of the wreckage from the sea. Further, grenades had to be exploded under the water to scare away the sharks. One diver had to be speedily pulled up to the surface when a shark got too near him.

The salvage ship of the Royal Navy H.M.S. *Barford* and the salvage ships of the Indonesian Navy were, between them, maintaining very good co-ordination and team work in the salvage operations.

As per the schedule drawn up by the Commission, its members would visit the site of the crash, along with representatives of the Embassy of the People's Republic of China in Djakarta, to assist in identifying the bodies of the members of the Chinese Delegation, when the bodies were recovered. The Deputy Director General and the Chief Inspector of Accident, Civil Aviation, Govt. of India, New Delhi, and the Divisional Operations Manager and Chief Inspector of Air India were already at the site of the crash supervising the salvage operations. In addition, the Director, Civil Aviation, Hong Kong, the Chief Investigating Officer, Ministry of Transport, and Civil Aviation, UK. and the Regional Service representative, Lockheed Aircraft Corporation, U.S.A. were also expected at the site of the crash within a short time.

The Prime Minister was satisfied and thanked me for briefing him on the progress of the investigations. The Prime Minister added that he should be kept informed of further developments in the matter, through

Mr. Tyabji. Thereafter, I clicked my heels, saluted smartly and left the room. The Prime Minister left Djakarta for New Delhi by air at 0900 hours on Wednesday, April 27.

ANNEXURE - 11

During the Asian-African Conference at BANDUNG in April 1955, Prime Minister Nehru had been receiving messages from the relations of the crew members of the ill-fated Air India International Constellatin Aircraft, *THE KASHMIR PRINCESS*, which crashed off the Great Natuna Islands on the 11th of April 1955. Nehru was extremely concerned, information about the fate of Captain Jatar and the other members of the crew. He had been informed earlier regarding the three survivors, CoPilot Dikshit, Flight Navigator Pthak and Aircraft Maintenance Engineer Karnik.

The note below from Camp Bandung was a result of this concern.

> I have seen several telegrams from Singapore and New Delhi regarding salvage operations of the Air India Constellation. Enquiry is made in this as to what the Indonesian Government is doing. What is the position? This is a very urgent matter, as delay will nullify any effort made. I presume you are in touch with the Indonesian Government.
>
> (J. Nehru)
> 18-4-1955.
> Camp: Bandung.
>
> Shri B.F.H.B. Tyabji.
> Colonel A. K. Mitra

ANNEXURE-12

COLONEL ON MISSION

Col. A. K. Mitra, Indian Military Attache in Indonesia, who arrived in Singapore yesterday.

Crash Inquiry Team Arrives In S'pore

Chapter 8

THE SALVAGE OF THE WRECKAGE

At 1330 hours on Thursday, April 28, 1955, the members of the Inquiry Commission alongwith Mr. K.M.Raha, Deputy Director General, Civil Aviation, India and four officials from the Chinese Embassy in Djakarta, boarded the Indonesian vessel The *Telantik* and sailed at 1500 hours.

She arrived at the site of the crash at 0800 hours on Sunday, May 1, 1955. Soon after arrival, the members of the Commission went aboard *H.M.S. Barford* and called on Commander Clark, who briefed the Commission regarding the progress of the salvage operations during the preceding two days. He said that great care was exercised while lifting the forward portion of the cockpit from the sea and unloading it on the top deck of the vessel. The body of the pilot, Capt Jatar, was found in the pilot's seat on the left side of the cockpit. The life jacket was on the body. The left arm was found entangled in a bundle of wires of the amplifier swinging mount. The condition of the surrounding structure was found to be intact. There were indications that his face had hit the instrument panel or windshield or some other object. His dress consisted of a white full-sleeved shirt with two pockets, a blue tie, and a badge of four stripes on the right shoulder, dark blue woolen trousers with two side pockets and one hip pocket and a leather girdle.

His skin was yellowish white. The skin on both hands and on the face was found peeled off. The skin at the eyebrow was found peeled off down to the bone. Both the eyes and the eyebrows, the nose and both lips were found smashed. In the lower jaw, four front teeth were missing but other teeth were intact. Two Indonesian doctors carried out an external medical examination of the body.

Keeping in view the condition of Capt Jatar's body, the Commander decided that the body should be transported immediately to Singapore for a post-mortem examination and cremation thereafter. The Commission decided that Mr. K.M.Raha and I should accompany the body to Singapore, along with two senior officials of the Indonesian Government and that the other members of the Commission and technical officers of the Govt. of India should stay behind at the site of the crash to supervise the salvage operations.

At about 1800 hours on Monday, May 2, 1955, Capt Jatar's body was placed in a special leadlined coffin and carried by Indonesian Naval personnel to the Indonesian Naval ship The Bajan. The coffin was draped in the Indian tri-colour, while the ensign of the ship flew half mast.

At 0800 hours on Wednesday, May 4, 1955, The Bajan reached Clifford Pier, Singapore. The coffin of Capt Jatar's body was unloaded from the ship into a launch in the presence of Mr. R.K.Tandon, Indian High Commissioner in Malaya, Dr. Horman Kartawisastro, Indonesian Consul-General at Singapore and Mr. R.N.Kaul, District Manager, Air India International, Singapore.

The body of Capt Jatar was removed to the mortuary in the Government hospital at Singapore and was later cremated at the Biradari Hindu Cemetery at Singapore on the same day.

On Tuesday, May 5, General Srinagesh, Chief of the Army Staff Designate of the Indian Army arrived at Singapore Port by vessel the *S. S. Chusan* on his way to India, after a short holiday trip to Hong Kong and Japan. I went and met him on board the ship at 0900 hours. The British Area Commander Maj. Gen. Tullock was also on board the ship to meet Gen. Srinagesh. I spent the entire day with General Srinagesh accompanying him to lunch, tea, cocktails and dinner hosted by various civil and military authorities. I briefed him about the crash of The Kashmir Princess and the results of the salvage operations. He sailed for India on Friday, May 6, 1955.

Thereafter I attended a meeting with Mr. Raha and other Indian officials regarding the future plans of the Inquiry Commission. Mr. Y. P. Malhotra, Inspector of Accidents, Civil Aviation, India and Mr. K.G. Appuswamy, Chief Inspector, Air India International Corporation, Bombay, who were supervising the salvage operations on board The ship *Barford* arrived in Singapore on Friday, May 6.

Great care had been taken during the salvage operations as a result of which 80% of the wreckage had been recovered. The only major structural component not recovered was the tail section. Little damage was caused during the operation of lifting of the different parts of the wreckage from the sea-bed and unloading them on to the top decks of the vessels. The salvage operations had been conducted under difficult conditions. Examination of different parts of the wreckage revealed that the aircraft had suffered considerable damage on impact with sea water, in addition to the damage caused by fire. The aircraft had broken into 12 major sections including cockpit, tourist section of the fuselage, rear section fuselage upto tail, port wing and starboard wing.

Disaster in the Air : The Crash of the Kashmir Princess 1955

As each broken section was recovered from the sea bed, they were individually examined by the two technical officers from India. The different parts of the wreckage had been taken to Djakarta.

Examination of different parts of the wreckage indicated that the fire had spread to the starboard side of the fuselage above the wing and had been of enough intensity to burn through the side of the fuselage. The fire had then spread to the cabin.

The starboard wing had been recovered by the Indonesian Naval vessel The *R. I. Triton* on April 30. The lifting gear on this vessel was unable to lift the starboard wing clear of the water and then unload it on the top deck of the vessel. Luckily the right wing which included the starboard wheel well had been recovered. Examination of the wheel well indicated evidence of explosion in that area. The nucleus of the explosion appeared to be at the centre of the wing and immediately forward of the rear beam. A hole had been blown through the bottom skin in that area and the surrounding skin had bulged outwardly. Pronounced and deep pitting, as if caused by shrapnel, had been detected on the surrounding skin, the site of strut assemblies and the steel drag link tube facing the explosion. The orientation of these pittings confirmed that the source of the explosion was in the wheel well area. The fuel tank well had been found punctured inwards. Further examination of the wreckage revealed positive evidence of an explosion in the starboard wheel well, set off by a "timed infernal machine", parts of which were found trapped in the wreckage. The explosion caused a puncture in fuel tank no. 3 resulting in the fuel gushing out and catching fire which spread rapidly.

The fact of the explosion in the starboard wheel well having been established, the two technical officers from India carried out a thorough and minute search of the entire area of the starboard wheel well by putting their hands into all accessible parts. This search resulted in the discovery of a "clockwork mechanism" which was found trapped between a corrugation and the rib forming the inner wall of the outer section of fuel tank no. 3. This mechanism had the "fast" and "slow" regulator graduation on it. Examination of the mechanism revealed that it had been subjected to heat, pressure and salt-water corrosion and that it was in no way connected with any equipment on the aircraft. As a result of further search, other parts forming part of the "clockwork mechanism" were also recovered.

The "clockwork mechanism" with a fast/slow regulator was despatched to Dr. Sugato, Director General, Civil aviation at Djakarta for safe custody. The other loose parts were left in the starboard wheel well which was packed in a gunny bag for further examination at a later date.

Message was sent to the Ministry of External Affairs, Govt. of India, New Delhi, through the Indian High Commissioner at Singapore conveying the above results, for the personal information of Mr. Nehru.

At 0845 hours on Saturday, May 7, the four of us (that is, Mr. K.M.Raha, myself and the two technical officers from India) left Singapore for Djakarta by Garuda Airways. We were received at the airport by some of the other members of the Inquiry Commission and we proceeded straight to the Ministry of Communications, to attend the conference convened by Dr. Sugato. Apart from the members of the Commission and other accredited representatives from India the others attending the conference were : Mr. M.J.Muspratt Williams, Director, Civil Aviation, Hong Kong, his adviser Mr. Newton, Chief Investigating officer, Ministry of Transport and Civil Aviation, Govt. of U.K., London and Mr. E.L.Duclos, Regional Service Representative, Lockheed Aircraft Corporation (of the U.S.A.).

Dr. Sugato informed all present about the progress of the salvage operations and the results obtained by the Commission till that time. It was decided to co-opt Mr. Muspratt Williams as the accredited representative of U.K. and Mr. Newton as his adviser. As the meeting was in progress, information was received that on the following day (that is, May 8) the Indonesian Naval vessel The *Gadja Laut* carrying certain parts of the wreckage, would be reaching Tandjung Priok Harbour, Djakarta. Before the meeting was adjourned, Dr. Sugato announced that after all the different parts of the wreckage of the aircraft salvaged from the site of the crash had arrived at Tandjung Priok Harbour and placed at the dock, all concerned would be advised to arrange for inspection and that such inspection may become possible by May 10.

Early in the morning on Sunday, May 8, the Indonesian Naval vessel The Gadja Laut, carrying certain parts of the wreckage of the aircraft, arrived and docked at Tandjung Priok Harbour, Djakarta. Mr. Alan Chaves was requested by the Chairman of the Commission to supervise the unloading of the parts of the wreckage.

On the morning on Monday, May 9, the members of the Commission and all other representatives from India, U.K. and Hong Kong attended a meeting in the office of Dr. Sugato . As the meeting was in progress, information was received that the Indonesian Naval vessel The Telantik, carrying certain other parts of the wreckage of the aircraft, was expected to dock at Tandjung Priok Harbour the following day, that is, May 10. Since May 10 was a holiday in Indonesia, the wreckage would be unloaded on May 11. Dr. Sugato informed Mr. Muspratt Williams, that as soon as all the parts of the wreckage of the aircraft had been received at Djakarta and are duly inspected and examined, the members of the Com-

Disaster in the Air : The Crash of the Kashmir Princess 1955

mission alongwith accredited representatives from India, would visit Hong Kong for an on-the-spot investigation. Mr. Muspratt Williams informed all those present at the meeting about the action taken by the Police authorities at Hong Kong to ensure the safety and security of the aircraft and of the members of the Chinese delegation on April 11, at Hong Kong Airport.

In the afternoon of Tuesday, May 11, the Indonesian Naval vessel The Blantik arrived at Tandjung Priok Harbour, with all the remaining parts of the wreckage of The *Kashmir Princess*.

Early next morning the members of the Commission along with other representatives of U.K. and Hong Kong, arrived at Tandjung Priok Harbour. The parts of the wreckage including the starboard wing with wheel well carried by The *Telantik* had still not been unloaded from the vessel and were still on board.

At the dock in the harbour, Mr. Imawan, Chairman of the Commission asked me to brief all those present at the dock about the various parts of the wreckage which had been salvaged and the findings of the Commission till that time. I informed the gathering that after the crash, the aircraft had broken into 12 major parts and examination of all those parts may take several days. To save time, it would be expedient to first examine the starboard wing and the wheel well where the explosion had taken place and objects that were found trapped in the wheel-well, because examination of these parts would certainly help solve the mystery of the crash of The *Kashmir Princess*. At that stage, Mr. Imawan, Chairman of the Commission, stated that the inspection of the various parts of the wreckage of the aircraft carried out by the Commission revealed positive evidence of an explosion in the starboard wheel well area, set off by a "timed infernal machine" parts of which were trapped in the wreckage and those parts were twisted, burnt and corroded. The "timed infernal machine" was a clockwork mechanism with a fast/ slow regulator graduation on it. It bore no relation to any other equipment of the aircraft and had been removed by the Commission and kept in safe custody in the building of the Ministry of Communications in Djakarta. The clockwork mechanism would be available for inspection by all those present at the dock that very afternoon.

Mr. Duclos, the Lockheed representative, proceeded to inspect the starboard wing and others also followed him. Mr. Duclos, while looking round the starboard wing, pushed his hand into the burnt-out space of the wheel well and pulled out some small unidentified parts and informed all present that those parts were in no way connected with any Lockheed Constellation aircraft equipment and, in his opinion, these appeared to be part of the clockwork mechanism. He was very happy about this discovery which confirmed that there was nothing wrong, technically or otherwise, with the aircraft the Lockheed Constellation, which crashed as a result of an act of sabotage.

All those present at the dock immediately left for Dr. Sugato's office in Djakarta to examine the clockwork mechanism.

The clockwork mechanism with an attachment plate and other small unidentified parts were shown to all members of the Commission as well as to their advisers by Dr. Sugato. After a thorough examination of the the timed infernal machine, all present were convinced that the ill-fated *Kashmir Princess* crashed as a result of an act of sabotage and not due to any other reason - a conclusion which was further corroborated by Mr. Muspratt Williams and Mr. Newton; the cause of the crash was definitely an explosion set off by the timed infernal machine (that is, the clockwork mechanism) which had been placed in the starboard wheel well of the aircraft.

That very afternoon at 1500 hours, all the members of the Commission and their advisers as well as other accredited representatives assembled in Dr. Sugato's office for another meeting. It was decided that the members of the Commission alongwith the two technical officers from India must forthwith proceed to Hong Kong for on-the-spot examination and interrogation of some crucial persons. It was decided that the Commission should leave Djakarta early morning the very next day for Hong Kong via Manila (Philippines). After a brief meeting at the British Embassy in Djakarta, Mr. Muspratt Williams and Mr.Newton decided to leave Djakarta for Hong Kong that very evening.

Engineer J.Heylingers, Air worthiness Section, Civil Aviation, Government of Indonesia (a member of the Inquiry Commission) and Mr. Y.R.Malhotra, and Mr. K.G.Appuswamy were entrusted with the responsibility of unloading the wreckage from The Talantik and to keep them in the shed in the Tandjung Priok Harbour and to carry out further examination of those parts of the wreckage.

ANNEXURE - 13

Flashback To Air Crash

Singapore Standard 5 May 55

THE body of Capt. D. K. Jatar, Commander of the "Kashmir Princess" which crashed in the South China Sea, being carried ashore from a launch at Singapore yesterday morning. At extreme left is Col. Mitra, who accompanied the body with Mr. K. M. Raha, a member of the Accident Investigation Commission.—Standard Photo.

BODY OF CAPTAIN REACHES COLONY

THE fifth victim to be found following the crash in the South China Sea of the Air India International Constellation, "Kashmir Princess," was its Commander, Capt. D. K. Jatar, whose body was brought to Singapore for cremation yesterday morning in the Indonesian Government ship Bajan.

It was recovered from the cockpit of the aircraft salvaged by the British naval ship H.M.S. Barford on May 1, and identified by the members and observers of the Accident Investigation Commission.

The body was borne ashore in a special lead-lined coffin by Indonesian ratings of the Bajan.

The coffin was draped with the Indian tricolour while the Bajan's ensign flew at half mast.

Two observers on the Commission, Mr. K. M. Raha, Deputy Director-General of Civil Aviation, Government of India, and Col. A. K. Mitra, India Government's Military Attache in Jakarta, arrived in Singapore with the body of Capt. Jatar.

Wreckage

More than 80 per cent of the wreckage has already been recovered from the sea. The Barford and the Indonesian navy ship Triton have jointly been responsible for the salvage operation.

"There has been perfect team-work between the two ships, and we are most grateful for the assistance they have given." Mr. Raha and Col. Mitra said.

The search of the sea bottom is still being continued by divers and by dragging.

Towards the end of this week, ships of the Indonesian Government will proceed to Jakarta with the wreckage, where it will be laid out for a close technical examination by experts of the Indonesian and Indian Governments and the Air India International.

CAPT. JATHAR DIED HERO'S DEATH

SINGAPORE, May 4.—The body of Capt. D. K. Jathar, pilot of Air India International's Kashmir Princess which crashed in the South China Sea off Sarawak on April 11, was brought to Singapore this morning by the Indonesian Liner Bijan.

Col. Mitra, military attache at the Indian Embassy at Djakarta, who accompanied the body to Singapore, told Press Trust of India that Capt. Jathar's body was found at the controls in the cockpit of the wrecked aircraft in a sitting posture showing that the pilot died at the post of duty.

Capt. Jathar's body and uniform were all intact and he died a hero's death, said Col. Mitra.

The body was received by Air India International's district manager here, Mr. R. N. Kaul, in a casket which was sealed and covered by a white cloth with the Indian tricolour on top.

Besides Col. Mitra, those accompanying the body were an Indonesian doctor Wunursto, an Indonesian official Raja Mohammed and Mr. K. M. Raha, Deputy Director-General of Indian Civil Aviation.

Those present at the Clifford pier when the body was brought in a launch from the Bijan included Mr. R. K. Tandon, India's High Commissioner in Malaya and the Indonesian Consul-General, Dr Herman Kartawisastra.

The body was removed to the mortuary in the Singapore Government Hospital. It is to be cremated at five this evening at the Bidadari Hindu Cemetery.—PTI.

ANNEXURE - 14 (A)

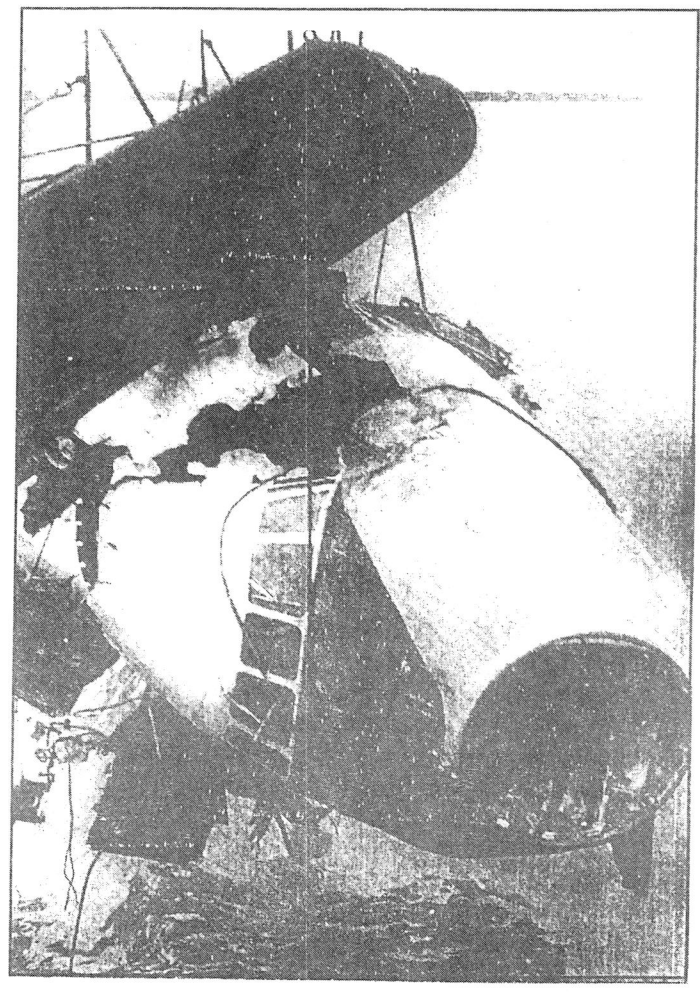

Front and port side - cockpit section

ANNEXURE - 14 (B)

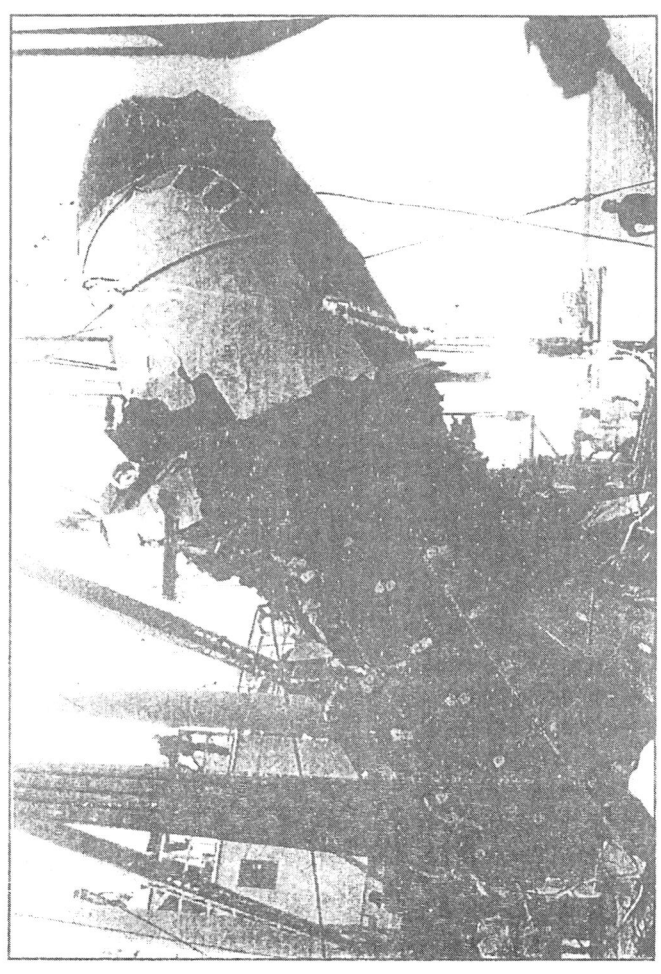

Top & Starboard Side

The Salvage of the Wreckage

ANNEXURE - 15(A)

Starboard Wing

ANNEXURE - 15 (B)

Outer wing bottom side star board wing

ANNEXURE - 16 (A)

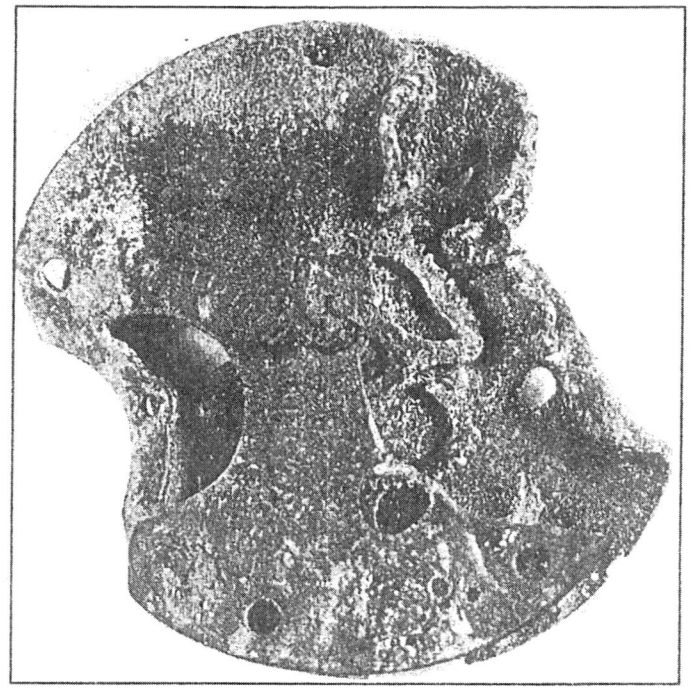

The twisted, burnt and corroded part of clock work-timed infernal machine with Fast / Slow Regulator graduation found trapped between a corrugation and rib forming the inner wall of No. 3 tank where the explosion took place.

ANNEXURE - 16 (B)

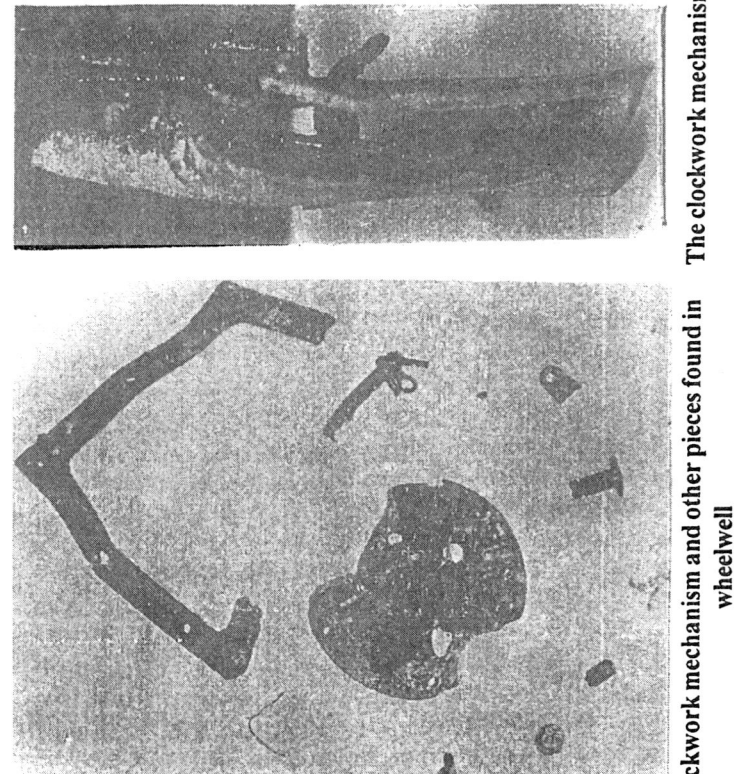

The clockwork mechanism

Clockwork mechanism and other pieces found in wheelwell

Chapter 9

THE MYSTERY OF THE CRASH UNRAVELLED AT HONG KONG

The Chairman of the Commission Mr. Imawan, other members of the Commission including myself, Mr. Alan J.Chaves, and others representing Indian and Indonesian aviation, left Djakarta at 0800 hours on Thursday May 12 for Hong Kong. At the stop-over at Manila, I called on my old friend Major Romalduz, earlier the Philippine Military Attache in Djakarta. The Chairman of the Commission Mr. Imawan and myself spent the evening with him as his guest and went around for sight-seeing.

Next day we flew on to Hong Kong, arriving there at 1600 hours, and were received by a representative of the Director General of Civil Aviation (D.G.C.A.), Hong Kong and the Indonesian Consul General in Hong Kong. The Kaitak Airport (Hong Kong) was sealed off for security reasons.

At 0900 hours on Saturday, May 14, the Chairman of the Commission, Mr. R.J.Imawan, accompanied by the Indonesian Consul General in Hong Kong presented his credentials to the Colonial Secretary of the Government of Hong Kong, who assured the Chairman that all facilities and co-operation would be extended to the Commission during their stay in Hong Kong. The Chairman of the Commission informed him that the Commission would commence interviewing concerned people from Monday May 16.

In the afternoon, the Commission met at the office of the Director of Civil Aviation, Hong Kong, Mr. M.J.Muspratt Williams. who informed the Commission that he had not yet obtained permission to release the details of the investigations carried out by the Hong Kong Security authorities. He added that he did not have the time to obtain other information, such as copy of the warning received from the British Embassy in Peking. However, he said that the Commissioner of Police and Chief of C.I.D of Hong Kong would be called to give to the Commission a brief resume of the actions taken till that time by the Hong Kong Police and would be glad to answer any questions put to them.

After due consideration, the Commission felt it inadvisable to interrogate separately the personnel screened by the Hong Kong Police and decided to confine themselves to the formal interrogation of the Acting Airport Manager, Hong Kong, Mr. F.R.J. Lillywhite on May 16. Mr. Lillywhite informed the Commission that he had been the Acting Airport Manager of the Hong Kong Airport since May 1954 and that his substantive designation and rank was Air Traffic Control Officer Incharge. In reply to the various queries made by the members of the Commission, Mr. Lillywhite deposed as follows :

Monday, April 11, 1955 was Easter Monday and was a public Holiday in Hong Kong. He was not on duty at the airport on that day. In his absence, the Deputy Aerodrome Control Officer or the Air Traffic Controller Incharge is usually the Officer Incharge of the Airport. Airport supervisors were also present at the airport to look after administrative matters. He added that visiting military transport aircraft are normally parked clear of the five bays. Therefore the U.S.A.F. aircraft were assigned to park outside the bay, whereas the Royal Air Force (R.A.F.) had their own parking place on the other side of the runway. Bays no. 1 and 2 were restricted to one-hour turn-round. Mr. Lillywhite confirmed that he had marshalling authority through the Air Traffic Control Officer in the control tower, but the tarmac marshalling was done by the staff of Hong Kong Aircraft Engineering Corporation (H.A.E.C.) at the parking bay assigned. The passengers had been driven right from the town up to the aircraft under arrangement with Hong Kong Police since the vehicle and the passengers had special permit passes.

Mr. M.J.Muspratt Williams, submitted a written note alongwith sketches and other details, to the Inquiry Commission, the text of which was as follows :

Circumstances prior to take-off at Hong Kong :

The Government of Hong Kong was informed over the weekend by telephone from her Majesty's Charge d' Affairs at Peking that the Chinese Ministry of Foreign Affairs had received information that trouble might be made by Chinese Nationalist sympathisers for a group of journalists leaving Hong Kong for Bandung Conference in an Air-India International plane. The Government was requested to take appropriate precautions. It was added that the Chinese Ministry of Foreign Affairs believed that the New China News Agency in Hong Kong would know where the journalists were staying and the time of their departure.

During the morning of Monday, 11 April, a representative of the New China News Agency telephoned to a senior police offcer to inform him that eleven journalists and a Vietminh delegate would be travelling by an Air India aircraft leaving Hong Kong early that afternoon. This aircraft had been chartered on behalf of the party by the China Travel Service Office in Hong Kong. No mention was made by the New China News Agency representative either then or later of any suspicion of trouble and the communication was made in a routine manner to which the Hong Kong authorities are now well-accustomed; But in the light of the message from the British Charge d'Affairs at Peking, steps were taken to provide extra security measures.

The plane came in on a schedule flight from India a few minutes after noon and was due to take off shortly after one 0'clock. Additional police precautions were taken to ensure that the party was not molested at the airport. During the time the plane was at the airport, it was under police guard under the command of an inspector. No unauthorised person was allowed to approach or board it. The Manager and other officials of Air India and crew members of the plane were present and supervised every aspect of refuelling and servicing. A member of the crew remained on board throughout. The actual handling of the luggage and passengers was done under the supervision of China Travel Service and senior officials of Air India.

The only articles placed aboard the plane in Hong Kong were 37 pieces of baggage (including two boxes of literature) belonging to the party and normal refreshments for passengers. The refreshments were supplied by a local firm but were checked on loading by a steward of the aircraft.

The passengers were brought to the airport by airline motor bus and exceptionally were taken straight to the plane without passing through Customs or Immigration. Similarly, without passing through Customs the luggage was loaded direct on to the plane under the supervision of Air India. Nothing else whatsoever was loaded on to the plane. The plane took off at about 1-26 pm (Hong Kong time) without incident.

Mr. Muspratt Williams began to make his statement before the Commission by reading out his written note of which he promised to hand over a copy to the Commission. He stated that since then a full interrogation and cross-examination of every person who, for whatever reason, might have been in the vicinity of the aircraft, had been going on. All people at the aerodrome had a pass issued after checks and screening had been made. Moreover, the people handling the aircraft were under supervision of the police. The aircraft was parked on no. 3 bay, nobody had access to it except personnel of Caltex, by whom refuelling was done, Shell who provided the oil, and Hong Kong Aircraft Engineering Corporation (H.A.E.C.) carried out maintenance work. A normal transit check was carried out, some special work was done on R.H. distributor of no. 2 engine. This detailed interrogation, which included also New China Travel Agency in Hong Kong, had not revealed anything. Mr. Muspratt Williams expressed his opinion that nothing could have been put into the aircraft at Hong Kong airport. He added that since all the areas of the aircraft were at a higher level, stands were required in order to reach nose wheel well, luggage compartments and engine bays. Mr. Muspratt Williams concluded that that was all he could tell the Commission, apart from his written note.

Replying to the queries of the members of the Commission, Mr. Muspratt Williams said that : the time of departure of the aircraft was about 13-26 hours. The aircraft was on the ground for 1 hour and 10 minutes between "Doors Open" and "Doors Closed".

The Chinese party had arrived in Hong Kong the Saturday before and had stayed in a special villa. As to how many persons of the staff of the organizations concerned with the handling of the aircraft actually attended to The *Kashmir Princess* at the Hong Kong airport on April 11, Mr. Muspratt Williams promised to obtain the exact information. He said that as far as he knew, they were all British subjects, their names and nationalities had been taken down. During the interrogation, the name of every person and his movements had been taken down.

In reply to the Commission's specific query as to who pulled the chocks out., Mr. Muspratt Williams stated that the information would be available in the records of the interrogation. He added that there were three entrances to the aerodrome guarded by Police posts. Anyone who wants to enter the tarmac area would have to have a permit. All the personnel of Hong Kong Aircraft Engineering Corporation (H.A.E.C.) have a pass issaed by Civil Aviation after verification by the police. There were some fifty-two people concerned with the handling of the aircraft. The office of the Director of Civil Aviation, Hong Kong, was in constant touch with the police which provided special guards. The airlines had their own guards. Some police guards were also deployed in the Aerodrome.

The Commission then interrogated Mr. P.F.Mehta, District Manager, Air-India International Corporation, Hong Kong, whose deposition was broadly as follows :

On the evening on April 10, the local representatives of New China News Agency in Hong Kong, who were looking after the arrangements for the chartering of the Air India plane for the Chinese Delegation, had contacted Mr. Mehta. He told the representatives about the rumours he had heard in Hong Kong that the members of the Chinese Delegation might probably be molested either on their way to the Hong Kong airport or at the airport. The local representatives of New China

The Mystery of the crash unravelled at Hongkong

News Agency (N.C.N.A.) felt that Mr. Mehta's statement was vague because they had heard of such rumours of threats of molestation and disturbance to the passengers from Communist China, particularly in connection with the chartering of the Air India plane for carrying representatives of Communist China from Hong Kong to other countries. Mr. Mehta, however, expected the local representatives of NCNA to take the usual precautions for the safety of the members of the Chinese Delegation. Mr. Mehta assured the representatives of NCNA that arrangements had been made for the transfer of the members of the Chinese Delegation direct to the aircraft as well as for obtaining normal Customs and Immigration clearances on Saturday, April 9, itself, instead of on Monday, April 11, the scheduled date of departure of the flight from Hong Kong to Djakarta. Mr. Mehta learnt that the representatives of NCNA would arrange to finalise with the office of Air-India the actual time-schedule as to when the Chinese Delegation should be picked up and taken to the aircraft and such other details.

At about 7.30 a m on the morning on April 11, the office of Air India in Hong Kong learnt that due to the delay in the departure of the aircraft from Bombay, the departure of the aircraft from Hong Kong would be some four hours behind schedule, i.e., 9.40 a.m. The representatives of NCNA were informed about the change in the departure time of the flight and were further told that as soon as further intimation was received from the aircraft they would be kept informed. According to Mr. Mehta's recollection, it was about 11-15 am (on April 11) that his office completed all arrangements and set the departure time of the flight as 1 p.m. (Hong Kong time). Mr. Mehta was present at the airport when the aircraft landed at about 12-10 pm on April 11, 1955.

After the Commander of the aircraft had deplaned, Mr. Mehta took him aside and apprised him of the rumours he had heard of threats of possible molestation and disturbance to the members of the Chinese Delegation and that in the interests of Air India all necessary precautions should be taken. Mr. Mehta asked the Commander if he could instruct the crew to check on everything themselves and he had specifically referred to refuelling and maintenance.

Air India had deputed a man to take delivery of the baggage of the members of the Chinese Delegation, at the air terminal and to mark each piece of baggage with white chalk and then load them into the aircraft. Another member of the staff of Air India was assigned to meet the passengers and to be with them until they boarded the aircraft. The coach drove straight up to the aircraft and all the passengers emplaned without delay.

Mr. Mehta made an overall check of the refuelling staff, catering staff and the mechanics supplied by Hong Kong Aircraft Engineering Corporation (H.A.E.C.) to ensure that there were no strangers about. As Monday April 11, was a pubic holiday in Hong Kong on account of Easter, the airport was deserted and no one went within 100 yards of the aircraft except the men on duty. The aircraft departed from Hong Kong at about 1-25 pm (Hong Kong time) on April 11.

At no time had any warning been received by the office of Air India in Hong Kong about possible sabotage to the aircraft. Subsequent to the crash of the aircraft on the evening on April 11, the following morning (that is, April 12) the Hong Kong Special Investigation Branch called on Mr. Mehta to take down his statement regarding the arrangements made by Air India in connection with the charter of their aircraft (that is, The *Kashmir Princess*) by the Government of the People's Republic of China. He told them of the statement he had received from the New China News Agency the previous day and the precautions taken by the office of Air India. In reply to the Commission's query, Mr. Mehta stated that there was no agency responsible for the loading of the luggage. This was handled by the handling agent of Air India, that is, Hong Kong Airways, under the supervision of the staff of Air India. The refuelling was done by Caltex with their usual team under the supervision of the Flight Engineer of the aircraft.

In reply to the Commission's query as to when he got the first message that something had gone wrong with the flight, Mr. Mehta replied that he received the news in the evening at about 8.35 pm (Hong Kong time) on April 11.

On the afternoon of Monday, May 16, the Commission called at Hong Kong Police Headquarters and met Mr. Maxwell, the Commissioner of Police and Mr. Wilcox, Chief of the C.I.D. The Chairman of the Commission, Mr. Imawan said that he was glad that the Hong Kong authorities were willing to provide all information to the Commission, relevant to their investigations. The Commissioner of Police requested all present that the discussions in his office and the information given should be kept strictly confidential by the Commission as otherwise it might prejudice further investigation by both the parties.

Mr. Imawan said that the Commission had learnt that a number of people connected with the movement of the aircraft, the movement of the baggage, the servicing of the aircraft and its refuelling, had already been screened by the police authorities but without any specific result. The Commission was, at that stage, in a position to provide the Commissioner of Police and the C.I.D. Chief with specific information as regards their findings in the wreckage to enable the Commissioner of Police and other security agencies in Hong Kong to proceed on more specific lines and narrow down the investigation. Mr. Imawan gave a brief resume of the activities of the Commission till that time. Interrogation of the three survivors at Bombay and Calcutta in India, and of other personnel in other organisations connected with the flight at Singapore and Djakarta. After salvaging of the wreckage and detailed inspection by technical officers from India, Hong Kong, U.K. and representative of the Lockheed Aircraft Corporation (in particular of the starboard wing and wheel well of the aircraft) there was irrefutable evidence of an infernal machine having been placed in the wheel well area where the explosion had taken place. The Commission was anxious to know the specific person responsible for the dastardly act of sabotage of the aircraft. The task of that person was rendered easier by the fact that access to that area was extremely easy through the openings in the bottom skin of the wheel-well, when the aircraft was on the ground. Mr. Imawan stated that the Commission suspected that the person employed by Haig's Maintenance Company was responsible for placing the infernal machine in the wheel well area, while removing the pins of the landing gear of The *Kashmir Princess* on that fateful afternoon of April 11, at Hong Kong airport.

Mr. Maxwell, the Commissioner of Police mentioned that they were under the impression, in the initial stages, that the trouble might have been caused at Bangkok. However, after hearing the findings of the Commission, they were convinced that the act of sabotage was perpetrated at Hong Kong airport. He informed the Commission that they had already screened and interrogated all the personnel employed at the airport and who were responsible for the handling of the aircraft. He added that they had already interrogated all the personnel of Haig's Maintenance Company including the person responsible for removal of the pins of the landing gear of the aircraft. He assured the Commission that they were keeping a close watch on all those persons and they would again try to find out the details of that particular person and inform the Commission the following day, that is, Tuesday, May 17. Mr. Imawan, after a brief meeting with the members of the Commission including Mr. Raha, decided that, after meeting the Commissioner of Police, in the afternoon of the following day (that is, May 17) all the members of the Commission should leave Hong Kong for Djakarta by the first available plane on Wednesday, May 18.

On the afternoon on May 17, 1955, the Commission called on the Commissioner of Police and the Chief of C.I.D., in the Commissioner's office. The Commissioner, Mr. Maxwell, and the C.I.D. Chief, Mr. Wilcox, looked very grim and worried. Mr. Maxwell said that he had very disappointing news to give to the Commission. Inspite of all the precautions taken, the concerned person (employee of Haig's Maintenance Company) who was manning the landing gear of the aircraft, had managed to sneak out of the security guards. According to the list provided by Haig's Maintenance Company, one Mr. Chu Chun Fai (a Canadian national of Chinese origin) was responsible for removing the pins of the landing gears of The *Kashmir Princess* on April 11, according to the laid-down procedures, just before the aircraft was to move to the take-off position. It was believed that Mr. Chu was smuggled out of Hong Kong on the night of 16th/17th May in the luggage compartment of an aircraft of the Air Transport Company to Formosa. The Air Transport Company was organised and run by a former General of the U.S.Army, whose headquarters was in Formosa. It was gathered that the Air Transport Company was mainly engaged in gun-running activities between Formosa and the outside world.

After hearing the shocking and disappointing news from the Commissioner of Police, the Commission made no comment. The Chairman of the Commission, Mr. Imawan, expressed his grateful thanks to the Hong Kong authorities for extending courtesy and co-operation to the Commission in their investigations and for the help rendered by Mr. Maxwell and Mr. Wilcox. Thereafter, all the members of the Commission departed from the offce of the Commissioner of Police, Hong Kong. The meeting with Hong Kong Police Commissioner on May 17, 1955 marked the conclusion of the Commission's investigations.

Chapter 10

THE COMMISSION'S FINDINGS

In order to determine the exact cause of the crash of The *Kashmir Princess*, the Commission had interviewed and interrogated the eye witnesses at the Port of Genting in Natuna Islands, the three survivors of the crash in Bombay and Calcutta in India, relevant personnel located in Singapore and Djakarta connected with the flight and the subsequent search and rescue operations. The Commission commenced its investigations on Thursday April 14 and concluded the investigations at Hong Kong on Tuesday May 17, that is over a period of 34 days.

With the advancement of technology, the aircraft manufacturers nowadays invariably equip their planes with the Flight Data and Cockpit Voice Recorder (called the Black Box). In fact, this is a mandatory requirement. In the earlier days (1950s and 1960s), the planes did not have the Black Box. The *Kashmir Princess* did not have a Black Box. However, the statements of the three survivors and the minute examination of the wreckage of the aircraft salvaged from the sea, helped the Commission in determining the exact cause of the crash.

An employee of Haig's Maintenance Company at Hong Kong, identified as Chu Chun Fai (a Canadian national of Chinese Origin), was responsible for removing the pins of the landing gears of The *Kashmir Princess* on April 11, just before the aircraft was to move to the take-off position. He had surreptitiously planted an explosive connected to a "timed infernal machine" in the starboard wheel well of the aircraft. The device exploded at about 5 pm on April 11, when the aircraft was flying over the Great Natuna Islands. The explosion punctured the fuel tank No. 3, resulting in highly inflammable fuel gushing out of the fuel tank. The fuel caught fire immediately and the fire spread rapidly and the entire aircraft was soon on fire, eventually leading to the crash of the aircraft into the sea. Parts of the "timed infernal machine" were found trapped in the wreckage.

That Chu Chun Fai was the saboteur was corroborated by the fact that he was smuggled out of Hong Kong in the midnight of 16th/17th May in the luggage compartment of an aircraft flying to Formosa, under the very nose of the Hong Kong Police and when the Inquiry Commission was in Hong Kong !

On the afternoon of Wednesday, May 18, Mr. Raha, Deputy Director General, Civil Aviation, Government of India, received a flash message from the Govt. of India, New Delhi, advising him to delay his departure from Hong Kong until he had met the Special Investigating Officer of the Govt. of India, Mr. Kaw, who was returning from Peking to Hong Kong on 18th May. Mr. Imawan, the Chairman of the Commission, felt that the entire Commission should wait in Hong Kong, so that additional information, if any, which Mr. Kaw might provide, could be duly taken into account by the Commission.

As scheduled, Mr. Kaw arrived in Hong Kong on 18th May. He had no additional information to provide to the Commission. He was anxious to get first-hand information on the findings of the Commission, which were conveyed to him.

While the Commission was anxious to fly back to Djakarta the next day, due to the non-availability of accommodation in any flight from Hong Kong to Djakarta, the Commission was unable to leave Hong Kong until Saturday May 21. The members of the Commission thus got two free days at Hong Kong which gave them time to do so some sight-seeing and shopping in Hong Kong. The members of the Commission called on Mr. Isak, the Indonesian Consul General in Hong Kong and thanked him for all the help and guidance given by him to the Commission.

In the forenoon on Saturday, May 21, the members of the Commission were seen off at Hong Kong airport by Mr. Muspratt Williams, Mr. Hamilton and the Indonesian Consul General. The members of the Commission boarded the Cathay Pacific Airways flight at 1200 hours and landed at Bangkok for a brief period, en route to Singapore. The flight landed at Singapore at 1930 hours.

On Sunday, May 22, Mr. R.K.Tandon, High Commissioner of India in Malaya invited the members of the Commission for lunch at his residence in Singapore and Mr. R.K.Kaul, General Manager, Air India International, invited the members of the Commission for dinner at his residence. The members of the Commission left Singapore at 0900 hours on Monday May 23, 1955 by BOAC flight which landed at Djakarta at 1130 hours the same day.

At 1700 hours on May 23, a meeting was arranged at Dr. Sugoto's residence. Dr. Sugoto gave details of the action taken at Djakarta by Civil Aviation authorities and Mr. Heyligers (nominated as the Secretary of the Commission who had remained in Djakarta while other members of the Commission were in Hong Kong). Mr. Imawan, the Chairman of the Commission, gave details of the interrogations, discussions and other activities which had taken place in Hong Kong and finally about the man who planted the explosive attached to a clock-work mechanism into the wheel well of the starboard wing of the aircraft and who managed to slip away from Hong Kong to Formosa.

Dr. Sugoto informed the Commission that the Prime Minister and the Minister of Foreign Affairs of Indonesia were scheduled to visit Peking on Wednesday, May 25, and therefore they were anxious that there should be no delay in the issue of a preliminary statement by the Commission giving the actual facts. While appreciating the urgency of issuing a preliminary statement, the Commission pointed out that it would be desirable to obtain the concurrence from both the Governments of India and the United Kingdom, before issuing such a statement.

While discussing the drafting of the report, it was unanimously decided that Mr. K.M.Raha, Deputy Director General, Civil Aviation, India, would help the Commission in finalising the draft of the preliminary statement, followed by the draft of the final report of the Commission.

At 0900 hours on Tuesday, May 24, the first meeting of the Drafting Committee took place in my office. Apart from Mr. K.M. Raha, the head of the Drafting Committee, the others present included Mr. Y.R.Malhotra, Chief Inspector of Accident, Civil Aviation, India, Mr. J. Heyligers, Airworthiness Section, Civil Aviation, Indonesia and myself. By afternoon the draft preliminary statement was finalised and this was later unanimously approved by all the members, representatives, advisers and by Dr. Sugoto with some minor amendments.

On Wednesday, May 25, a final conference was held at the office of the Minister of Communication of Indonesia, Mr. A.K.Gani, and attended by the members of the Inquiry Commission and Mr. B.F.H.B. Tyabji, the Indian Ambassador. The Minister observed that in order to prevent undesirable rumours spreading before the finalisation of the Commission's report, it would be desirable for the Govt. of Indonesia to issue the statement immediately. There was some objection from the Indian Ambassador but after further discussions, it was agreed that the Preliminary Statement may be issued at 0001 hours on Friday, May 27, simultaneously in Djakarta, New Delhi, Hong Kong and London, after the concurrence of the respective Governments.

On the evening on Wednesday May 25, the Indonesian Cabinet discussed the preliminary report of the Inquiry Commission. The meeting was presided over by the Deputy Prime Minister of Indonesia, Mr. Zainul Arifin. The text of the Communique issued by the Govt. of Indonesia was as follows :

"The Council of Ministers, Government of Indonesia, held its weekly session in the evening of May 25, 1955. The meeting heard and discussed the Preliminary Report of the Communication Ministry on the crash of the Air-India Super Constellation Kashmir Princess in the waters near Natuna Islands on April 11, 1955. It was decided that the Preliminary Report be published next Friday 27th May.

The Findings

The Inquiry Commission handed over its report with findings and comments to the Government of Indonesia on May 25, 1955. The Commission's findings were summarised as under :

Cause

The Commission determined that the cause of this accident was an explosion of a timed infernal machine, placed in the starboard wheel well of the aircraft.

This explosion resulted in puncturing of no. 3 fuel tank, and an uncontrollable fire.

Comments on the cause of the accident

The aforementioned facts provide irrefutable evidence, presumably to destroy the aircraft. The task of the person was rendered easier by the fact that access to the area was extremely easy through the opening in the bottom skin of the wheel well, when the aircraft was on the ground. It was clear that the explosion was followed by a combination of circumstances which embraced practically all emergencies that the crew could have faced. A serious fire that threatened to burn off the wing any minute, hydraulic failure, electrical failure, partial loss of control and dense smoke in the cockpit which restricted the visibility to almost nil during the most critical stages of the descent.

On the conclusion of the work of the Inquiry Commission set up by the Government of Indonesia to inquire into the crash of the Air India plane, *Kashmir Princess,* I issued the following statement to the press to express thanks, on behalf of the Embassy of India and the Government of India, to the Indonesian authorities :

"As accredited representative of the Government of India on the Commission set up by the Indonesian Government to enquire into the fatal accident to the Air India International Constellation, VT-DEP *"Kashmir Princess"* on Monday 11th April, 1955, off the Natuna Islands I had an opportunity to observe great help given to the Commission on their investigation, by the Indonesian Air Force, Indonesian Navy, the Directorate of Civil Aviation and the Civil officials and population of the Natuna

The Commission's Findings 113

Islands".

Airforce Efforts (AURI)

As soon as the distress signal of the *Kashmir Princess* was received at about 5 pm on the 11th" April in Djakarta, the Chief of the Indonesian Air Force, Air Vice Marshal Suryadarma, lost no time in despatching a DC 3 (Dakota) for a night take-off to reach the scene of the accident soon after daybreak. A Catalina (flying boat) was also alerted to take off in the early hours of the 12th" April, 1955. In view of the absence of navigational and night landing facilities in the archipelago, this was indeed a creditable effort.

"I should like particularly to mention the co-operation of the AURI in placing a Catalina plane entirely at the disposal of the Commission. I should also like to congratulate the Captain of the Catalina PBY - 505 for the special skill and daring in landing and taking off the aircraft in uncharted waters time and again inspite of the fact that the RAF Sunderland considered it a dangerous operation for landing.

"The Indonesian Navy (ALRI), inspite of their operational commitment, moved a number of naval ships from the various ports of Indonesia to the scene of the accident, without any loss of time, to assist in the search for survivors and in salvaging the wreckage. The cooperation between the Indonesian Navy and Air Force and the British Navy and the Royal Air Force also helped towards the speedy location of the wreckage and its salvage.

"The Directorate of Civil Aviation of the Indonesian Government spared no pains in setting up quickly a Commission of Inquiry. It was because of the fact that the Commission consisted of such experienced Indonesian officials, that the investigation was completed successfully in such a short time".

"Gratitude

I should like, however, to thank particularly the civil officials of the local administration in the Natuna Islands and the Captains of the Bajan, Balantik and Triton who provided the Commission with all facilities for the work in Natuna Islands. The way the villagers and Islanders co-operated in investigation not only as eye witness account of the accident but also affording facilities for the burial rites of some of the unfortunate victims, was also praiseworthy "The Government of Indonesia afforded all facilities to the Indian members of the Commission to carry out their task successfully. Special mention should be made to the action of the Government of Indonesia in placing at the disposal of the Indian members of the

Commission, S.S.Bajan to carry Captain Jatar's body from the Natunas to Singapore for burial".

ANNEXURE - 17

THE PLANE WAS SABOTAGED

Causes of crash of Kashmir Princess to be published Friday?

Djakarta, May 25.

According to information obtained by Antara, the causes of the crash of the Air India constellation "Kashmir Princess" off the Natuna islands may be made public Friday, May 27th.

The "Kashmir Princess" Enquiry Committee has arrived back in Djakarta from its observation visit to Hongkong and today it held a meeting at the Ministry of Communication. Besides members of the Enquiry Committee the meeting was attended by the Minister of Communications, Indian Ambassador in Djakarta, Tyabji and others.

Up to the writing of this report not one of the Committee members was prepared to disclose the results of their investigation. In this connection the Minister of Communications, A. Gani only said, that up to the present no conclusion could be drawn from the investigations conducted by the Committee, adding that the Committee's report on its investigations may be completed next Friday and may also be published the same day.

The Indonesian Enquiry Committee is scheduled to hold another meeting on Friday.

As is known the "Kashmir Princess" crashed in Indonesian waters off the Natuna islands while on its way to Djakarta from Hongkong carrying several members of the Chinese delegation to the Asian-African Conference.

Cabinet discusses question of "Kashmir Princess"

The Council of Ministers held its weekly session Wednesday evening discussing the question of the crash of the "Kashmir Princess" and security problems. The meeting was presided over by deputy Prime Minister Zainul Arifin.

Following the meeting Information Minister Tobing was not prepared to attend to the press but passed merely to the communiqués issued by the Cabinet.

Communiqué

The communiqué runs as follows:

"The Council of Ministers has held its weekly session in the evening of May 25, 1955.

"The meeting heard and discussed the preliminary report of the Commission of Ministers on the crash of the Air Indian Super-Constellation 'Kashmir Princess' in the waters near Natuna islands on April 11, 1955.

Kashmir Princess sabotaged

By our correspondent

It has been decided by the Investigation Committee of the Kashmir Princess crash that the accident was due to sabotage. This was revealed today by the Investigation Committee. The statement which was announced this morning by the Ministry of Communications said that the cause of the accident was due to an explosion of a time bomb, found in the right-hand side wheel of the craft. The gasoline tank number three caught fire. The remains of the time bomb are still in the plane, and are definite proof of the already planned explosion.

The Investigation Committee is composed of M. Imawan, Mr. Soetomo, Mr. Heiligers, all three of the Department of Civil Aviation, and Mr. Kamminga, head of the Operations service of the Garuda Indo-

timebomb in plane

nesian Airways. This statement was also signed by Mr. K.M. Raha, deputy Secretary General of Civil Aviation India, Colonel A.K. Mitra, Military Attaché of the Indian Embassy in Djakarta, and Mr. A.R. Malhotra, inspector of accidents of Civil Aviation India. The British Government in the committee is represented by Mr. M.J. Musprat-Williams, head of Civil Aviation Hongkong and Mr. Newton officer of the Ministry of Transportation and Civil Aviation in London. Technical advisors in the Committee are Mr. Chaves, ICAO mission in Indonesia, Captain R. Vishwanath, divisional operations manager All India International Corporation - Bombay, K.G. Appusamy, inspector of Air India International Corporation, Bombay, and Mr. Duclos, regional service representative Lockheed Aircraft Corporation.

Chapter 11

TRIBUTES TO THE VICTIMS, THE SURVIVORS AND THE RESCUERS

The oral statements of the three survivors, Captain M.C.Dikshit, Co-Pilot, Mr. J.C.Pathak, Flight Navigator, and Mr. A.S.Karnik, Aircraft Maintenance Engineer, revealed that Captain D.K.Jatar, the Pilot and Commander of the ill-fated *Kashmir Princess* had remained calm and kept his cool right from the time it was reported to him that the starboard wing of the aircraft was on fire upto the time the aircraft eventually crashed into the sea off Natuna Islands on April 1 l, 1955. It was obvious that his main concern was to save the lives of the passengers and the crew, since he held on to the controls of the aircraft till the very end. He had thus displayed extraordinary courage inspite of the great personal danger to himself and exceptional devotion to duty. He had literally died in harness. Till the end, he had maintained the highest traditions of a true leader and had died a hero's death.

The Commission was told by the Air India authorities at Bombay that 23 year old airhostess, Miss Gloria Berry, had volunteered to go on duty on the *Kashmir Princess* as it gave her an opportunity to do some shopping at Hong Kong as she was going to be married shortly. Unfortunately, she became one of the victims of the crash of the ill-fated *Kashmir Princess* . Immediately after the distress message "MAY DAY" was sent by the aircraft, she rushed about helping the passengers and the crew with life jackets and attending to other emergency duties. She ensured that the Captain and the Co-Pilot Dikshit put on the life jackets. Captain Dikshit said that Miss Berry not only brought the life jacket to him but also insisted on his wearing it immediately and she had thus saved his life and he would ever remain grateful to her. She had displayed exceptional courage, and presence of mind in the face of great personal danger to her life and rendered selfless service to all the passengers and the crew thereby keeping up the highest traditions of her profession. Inspite of all efforts, the divers could not find her body.

The three surviving members of the crew, M/s Dikshit, Pathak and Karnik displayed extraordinary courage, will power and stamina by extricating themselves from the crashed aircraft from the depths of the sea to the surface of the water where they were surrounded by burning fuel on the surface of the water. They tried to help each other to escape from the burning fuel. They kept on swimming and floating in the sea for more than five hours in darkness and under the most trying conditions. The sea was rough. It was raining and the weather was cold in the open sea and there was a sudden outbreak of a storm. It was their sheer will power and courage that helped them to survive and pass through such a traumatic experience.

The five Indonesian islanders who had helped in rescuing the three surviving members of the crew of the ill-fated *Kashmir Princess* Natuna Islands on April 12, 1955, were duly honored for their exceptional humanity, as will be evident from the news item and photographs appearing at the end of this chapter.

Tributes to the Victims, the Survivors and the Rescuers 119

ANNEXURE - 18
Page 1

Ceremony held at the NEGARA PALACE, Djakarta on February 22, 1956

Address delivered by Mr. B.F.H.B. Tyabji, Ambassador of India, on the occasion of the Presentation of Awards from the Government of India to Indonesian islanders who helped in the rescue of the survivors of the "Kashmir Princess" Air Disaster.

Mr. President, Excellencies, Ladies and Gentlemen,

This is an occasion capable of rousing mixed feelings in many of us present here today. You have all heard of the ill-fated Indian International airliner, the "Kashmir Princess", which crashed in flames on the 11th April 1955, in Indonesian waters. All its 11 passengers - of whom 9 were Chinese delegates to the Asian-African Conference, - along with its Captain and 7 members of the crew, suffered a horrible and agonizing death. Their death was caused by one of the most inhuman crimes committed in recent International history. If I dilated on it, it might make one despair of the capacity of contemporary man to evolve into a human member of a World Society. But as frequently happens, when one's despair is greatest about the nature of man, he exhibits qualities which again stir in one, one's faith in man's unconquerable spirit in his struggle to attain divinity.

ANNEXURE - 18
Page 2

I stand here today not to spread despair nor to arouse hatred; but to re-affirm our belief in man's humanity and his will to serve his fellowmen.

I submit that we cannot do this better than by honouring these Indonesian islanders; whom you, Sir, have invited us to meet this morning; and whose deeds, with your permission, will briefly be recounted for the benefit of those who do not yet know how well they have fulfilled all the ideals of fraternal behaviour in utter disregard of their own personal safety.

The President of India, on our Republic Day the 26th January-this year, has already conferred the posthumous decoration of Ashoka Chakra Class I on the gallant Captain Jathar of the "Kashmir Princess", who lost his life attempting till the last to save the aircraft, its passengers and crew from the fate which he knew would overtake them, if he lost his nerve or thought only of saving himself. The Ashoka Chakra is one of the highest decorations which India can bestow on her own nationals for bravery and seflessness.

Here, I might also mention the heroism displayed by the other members of the crew and by the young Air Hostess who, each in their turn, displayed a devotion to duty and considerateness for others which was in the highest traditions of the Chivalry of the Air.

The only survivors from the aircraft were three members of its crew, Messrs. Dixit, Karnik and Pathak. In their escape from the disaster and subsequent welfare as well as in the salvage and location of the wreckage, the Indonesian islanders whom we have met to honour today, played a leading role.

I now crave your permission, Sir, to present these Indonesians a token of high appreciation which the Government and the people of India have for the outstanding gallantry and humanity which they displayed on that occasion.

	Name	Address	Remarks		
1.	MUSA	Ajer Nali Klari, Pulau Bunguran Barat, Great Natuna Islans.	Age Occupation	: :	18 Yrs. Farmer
2.	WAN SABAN	Pulau Batu Bilis, Great Natuna Islands.	Age Occupation	: :	50 Yrs. Farmer

ANNEXURE - 18
Page 3

3.	MADJUN	Klari, Plau Bunguran Barat, Great Natuna Islands.	Age Occupation	: :	40 Yrs. copra trader
4.	SAID HAMZAH	Pemimpin Balai Pengobtan Bunguran Barat Soedanan Island	Age Occupation	: :	i/c Clinic
5.	Assistant to SAID HAMZAH	— do —	Age Occupation	: :	Asstt. in Clinic

ANNEXURE-19

Duta besar India

Serahkan tanda djasa pada rakjat pulau Natuna jang menolong „Kashmir Princess"

Didalam satu upatjara jang telah dilangsungkan di Istana Negara di Djakarta pada hari Rebo tanggal 22 Pebruari, Duta besar India. Tuan B.F.H.B. Tyabji, menjerahkan medali-medali jang istimewa dibikin dan hadiah sedjumlah uang kontan kepada kelima orang Indonesia penghuni pulau-pulau jang telah memberikan bantuannja didalam menjelamatkan orang-orang jang tertolong dari pesawat udara India. „Kashmir Princess" jang telah djatuh diperairan Indonesia pada tahun jl. Gambar menundjukkan kedua-belah muka dari medali itu, jang diserahkan pada upatjara tersebut. Tulisan diatas medali itu berbunji: „Untuk Keperwiraan dan kemanusiaan jang telah ditundjukkan terhadap orang-orang jang tertolong dari pesawat udara India „Kashmir Princess" jg telah djatuh diperairan Indonesia pada tanggal 12 April 1955."

At an elaborate ceremony to be held at President's Palace in Djakarta on Wednesday, February 22, the Indian Ambassador, Mr. B.F.H.B. Tyabji, presented specially struck medallions and cash awards to the five Indonesian islanders who helped in the rescue of survivors from the Indian airliner "Kashmir Princess" which crashed in Indonesian waters last year.

The photograph shows the two sides of the medallions which is to be presented to each of the five islanders at the ceremony. The inscription on the medallion reads: "For gallantry and humanity shown to the survivors of the Indian airliner "Kashmir Princess" which crashed in Indonesia waters on 12.4.55".

ANNEXURE-20(A)

HONOURING THE INDONESIAN ISLANDERS

MUSA, WAN SABAN, MADJUNE SAID HAMZA rescued the three survivors after the crash of Air Indian Constallation "Kashmir Princess" of Natuna Islands on 12th April, 1995.

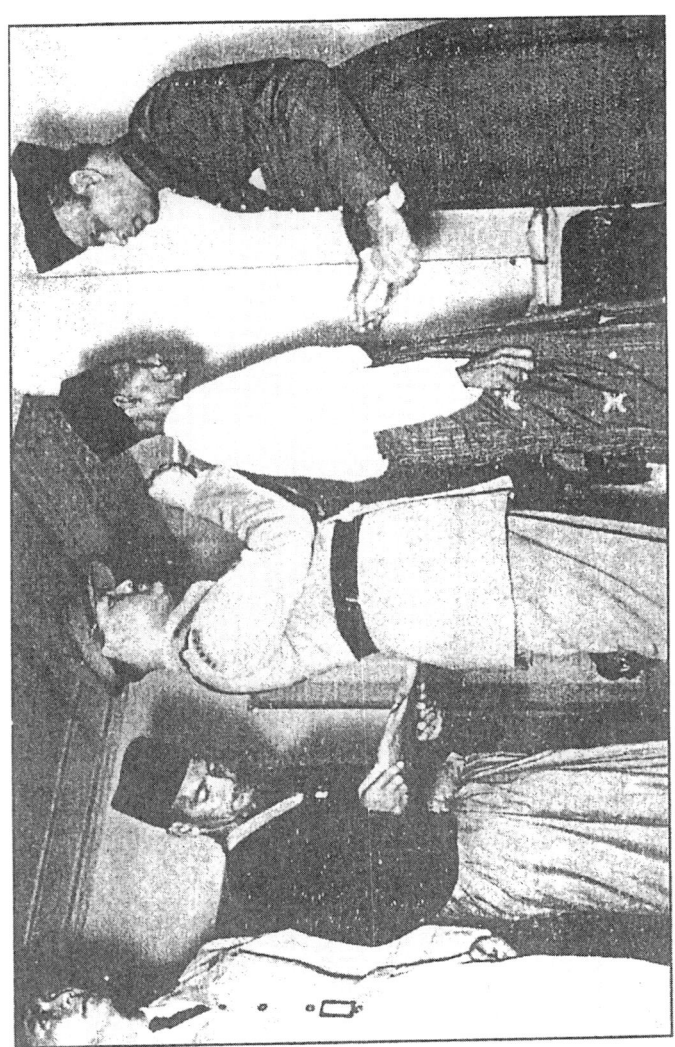

At President's Palace, Djakarta, at the presentation ceremony on February 22nd, 1956, the Ambassador of India Mr. Tyabji, presented specially struck medallion and cash awards to the Islanders from Natuna. Colone MITRA is helping the Ambassador.

ANNEXURE - 21

MARDEKA PALACE (October — 1955)

Colonel and Mrs. A. K. Mitra with Dr. Soekarno at the palace.